THE LOST RAILWAYS
OF
LINCOLNSHIRE

Day trippers arriving at Mablethorpe, about 1930 (see Chapter Ten)
Courtesy Grimsby–Louth Railway Preservation Society

The Lost Railways

of

Lincolnshire

Stewart E Squires

CASTLEMEAD PUBLICATIONS
WARE

First Published in 1988

CASTLEMEAD PUBLICATIONS
Swains Mill, 4A Crane Mead
Ware, Herts., SG12 9PY
Publishing division of
WARD'S PUBLISHING SERVICES

ISBN 0 948555 14 9

© Stewart E Squires 1988

British Library Cataloguing in Publication Data

Squires, Stewart E.
    The lost railways of Lincolnshire.
    1. Lincolnshire. Railway services, 1848–
1986
    I. Title
    385'.09425'3

ISBN 0–948555–14–9

Printed in Great Britain in
10pt Palatino Roman Type
by Anchor Brendon Limited, Tiptree, Essex

Foreword

It has long been my wish that a book describing all the many railway lines in the vast and fascinating County of Lincolnshire might be published. So I have much pleasure in writing the foreword to Stewart Squires' most welcome volume. Not only are the various lines of the large railway companies described, together with some of their less well known branches, but also lines of private undertakings which have not before received the attention they deserve. There are many excellent illustrations to focus attention of the reader and revive memories of any who were acquainted with the county.

Although I have never had direct associations with Lincolnshire I did spend a great deal of time in my early years in the Soke of Peterborough, some three miles outside the Lincolnshire boundary. I retain pleasant memories of frequent trips over the East Lincolnshire line, sometimes by the early morning all stations train from Peterborough to Grimsby. Noting *en route* the imposing Boston Stump and also the lovely floral display at Aby where the devotion of the staff was rewarded many times in LNER days with First Prize in the annual Station Gardens competition. Then there was an exciting ride from Grimsby to Cleethorpes on the top deck of a tram with open canopies at each end.

Some holidays were spent at Mablethorpe and Skegness where I once spent a Saturday afternoon at the station keenly watching the intensive traffic mostly handled by locomotives built by the old Great Northern Railway. Nearby was an important railwayman in his capacity of District Superintendent, Lincoln, watching every operation closely. He was Mr

G Sutcliffe who had risen from the ranks and had earlier been Stationmaster at Peterborough and King's Cross, London. He was Lincolnshire born and was respected by all who came in contact with him. Other days were spent at Spalding where a constant procession of trains passed through, to and from the marshalling yards at March, as well as the noted 'North Country Continental' boat express from Harwich to Liverpool. The ancient locomotives of the Midland and Great Northern Joint Railway gave added interest. These short journeys were facilitated by using Market tickets on Tuesdays at a modest cost.

Only those who have actually lived in Lincolnshire or spent periods of time there really appreciate it's true atmosphere. Undoubtedly there has always been a dearth of written information about the many railway systems in the County. I was once impelled to take to task the well-known writer on railway matters, Cecil J Allen, for describing a journey over the East Lincolnshire line as 'Through the wilds of Lincolnshire'. Nothing could be further from the truth!

Many people will glean much knowledge from this book. In particular about the Cranwell Railway, the ironstone railways and Bawtry to Haxey, none of which have been adequately described or illustrated before and therefore not well known outside their localities. The author is to be congratulated on his painstaking work in compiling a comprehensive account of the many railways which have now gone for ever.

Eric Neve
Bedford, May 1988

Acknowledgements

The most rewarding aspect of writing this book has been the help I have received from so many people, mainly, but not only, from the geographical area covered, which has sustained my interest and enthusiasm over the many months it took to prepare.

I have corresponded with, and spoken to, people of all ages and walks of life; serving and retired railwaymen, amateur photographers, local historians, railway enthusiasts, and people who just wanted to help. They have given me their time and to add flesh to the bones of my own knowledge. I owe them all a great debt of gratitude and I have listed their names below. I am particularly grateful to two people worthy of special mention, Ray Robinson, for much of the photographic work, and my wife, Julie, for her help and support.

I believe all the information to be correct, but any errors which may be found in text or map, are mine alone.

I would be interested to hear of any additional photographs, facts or other material for incorporation in future publications.
Particular thanks are due to the following:

Glenn Answer	Peter Grey	Ray Robinson
H L Answer	M Hall	G R Rowe
M Back	J Hickling	E Squires
Ralph Bates*	R Hooley	E Steele
R Bones	J E Hurton	B Stephenson
R E Burdon	Ron Knight*	Stephenson Locomotive
Mrs A Campion	Ralph Kitson	Society
P Carter	Paul Lefevre	P Sutton
W Gordon Clark	Tim Mawson	D Swift
H Davies	R K McKenny	D Thompson
G Dow*	E Neve	B Walster
L R Durham	G Nightscales	Doris Waters
J Edwards	G W Parkinson	M White
G Flatters	B Peeps	
Richard Goodman	Jim Radley	* Now deceased

viii

Contents

List of Maps

Introduction

The British have a fascination with their rural railways and care about what happens to them. The evidence can be seen in the local outcry when one is threatened, the many privately restored sections of line along which, often, steam trains run again, or the former routes now used by the cyclist and rambler. Even today, twenty years after complete dieselisation of the national network, with few really rural branch lines remaining, our children's books and magazines have stories of tiny steam tank engines running along often overgrown rails in deep rural areas.

The railway is fascinating because of the way it revolutionised the lives of our Victorian ancestors, for the way it altered forever the isolation of those who lived in the countryside – the countryside it changed the face of with its buildings and earthworks. At the height of the railway age it is said that no town or village in England was more than twenty miles from a station.

Prior to its coming, most of the rural population were born, lived and died within their communities, very rarely travelling outside a few miles radius of their home. Coach travel was expensive, and so they were limited to where they could walk, or travel by the local carrier's cart. The railway opened up tremendous opportunities – employment, cheap travel, a variety of destinations, cheaper prices, country markets for the growing industries it stimulated in the towns, and town markets for the products of the countryside. It also took the young on the first steps of their adult life, away to the towns to work, off to war, or to emigrate to new lands overseas. Invariably, almost all lines opened with flags, speeches and bands playing.

Compton Mackenzie wrote, prophetically, in *The Darkening Green*, for when it was published in 1934 there were very few disused railway stations to be found

> . . . The small country railway stations . . . have contrived not merely to avoid insulting the landscape, but in many cases actually to add something to it. In the far future, when they cease to serve man's purpose, their platforms covered then by grass

will no doubt diffuse a magical atmosphere like the still discernible contours of Roman camps. The site of an old railway station will be a nook for lovers to dream away secluded a summer's afternoon on the springy turf that will have covered the permanent way. Many of the roads that lead to the stations, their utility outlived, will become grassy tracks avoided by motorists. And if emotion has in truth the power to affect a place with that atmosphere we call haunted, surely the sites of old railway stations will be the most haunted spots of all – railway stations where parted so many mothers and sons, so many husbands and wives; so many lovers and so many friends; railway stations up and down whose platforms the fugitive from justice, the fortune seeker, the exile and the emigrant have fearfully paced; railway stations with their overwhelming sorrows and their equally overwhelming joys . . .

The network grew from the 1830s until around the time of the First World War. Contraction started, very slowly at first in the late 1920s, culminating with the main closures of the 1960s, the well known Beeching era. This has left ribbons of part reclaimed, part overgrown, land threading its way through the British countryside.

Certainly since the Second World War, closures have been celebrated with due ceremony, trains full with people from near and far taking their last journey, wayside stations with their knot of local people watching the last train pass by, some with bands playing and flags at half mast. They say there is nothing new under the sun, and indeed, similar celebrations attended the last runs of the long distance coaches between 1830 and 1850, as they were replaced by the iron road.

The title of this book could be taken to be a misnomer, as I have included lines south of the River Humber which are now

'. . . their platforms covered then by grass will no doubt diffuse a magical atmosphere.'

Withcall Station, after a short, sharp, summer shower in 1985. This tiny waiting room is still in use today as a Methodist chapel. The site of the signal box can be seen in the foreground, a hole in the platform through which passed the rodding

© Author

xii

in South Humberside. However, up to 1974 they were all in Lincolnshire, hence the title. In addition, for the sake of convenience, where closed lines cross the county boundary I have written about them to the first convenient town, village or junction in adjoining counties.

In Lincolnshire and South Humberside there are 334 miles of former standard gauge railway lines along which no trains now run. This includes twenty-seven miles of ironstone railways, fifteen miles of rural tramways, and five miles built by the Admiralty – twenty-five miles from the sea.

The area has always been relatively sparsely populated. It has a great agricultural and engineering tradition, and it was for these reasons, to transport grain, vegetables, fruit and manufactured goods as well as the people, that the railways first came, and the reason for so many goods services remaining after lines lost their passenger trains.

The first line into the area reached Lincoln in 1846, and additional lines followed until the last major railway develop-

ment in 1913. However, only twelve years later rationalisation began with the first major closure brought about not by competition from other railways, as previous closures had been, but by competition from the roads.

Although not all routes were successful in use, they cannot be said to be of no use now and for this reason I hesitate to use the word 'disused' to describe them. Many miles have been incorporated into adjoining fields or are used as farm tracks, station and level crossing houses are still lived in, yards are used by a variety of commercial concerns, and the rest provides a home for wild plants, animals, birds and insects.

For some reason the railway history of Lincolnshire and South Humberside is much less well documented than most other areas of the country. More recently, authors have begun to redress the balance. This book, I hope, fills a gap in the knowledge, but as it is largely about birth and death, much remains to be written about life.

Lincolnshire Railways – northern area

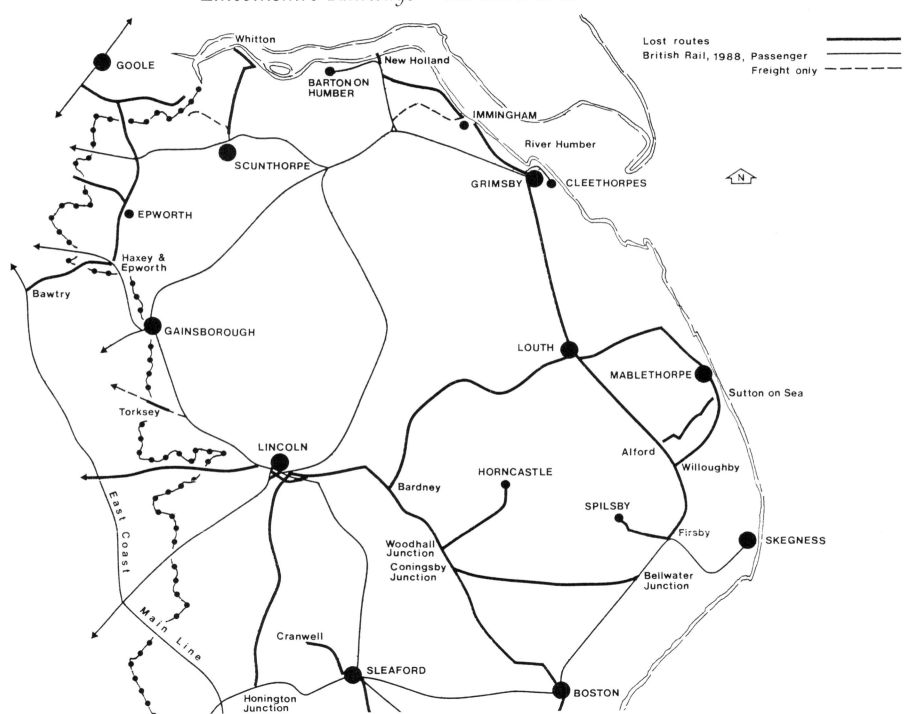

Lost routes

British Rail, 1988, Passenger

Freight only

Whitton

GOOLE

New Holland

BARTON ON HUMBER

IMMINGHAM

River Humber

SCUNTHORPE

GRIMSBY

CLEETHORPES

N

EPWORTH

Haxey & Epworth

Bawtry

GAINSBOROUGH

LOUTH

MABLETHORPE

Sutton on Sea

Torksey

Alford

Willoughby

LINCOLN

HORNCASTLE

Bardney

SPILSBY

Firsby

East Coast

Woodhall Junction

Coningsby Junction

Bellwater Junction

SKEGNESS

Main Line

Cranwell

SLEAFORD

Honington Junction

BOSTON

Lincolnshire Railways – southern area

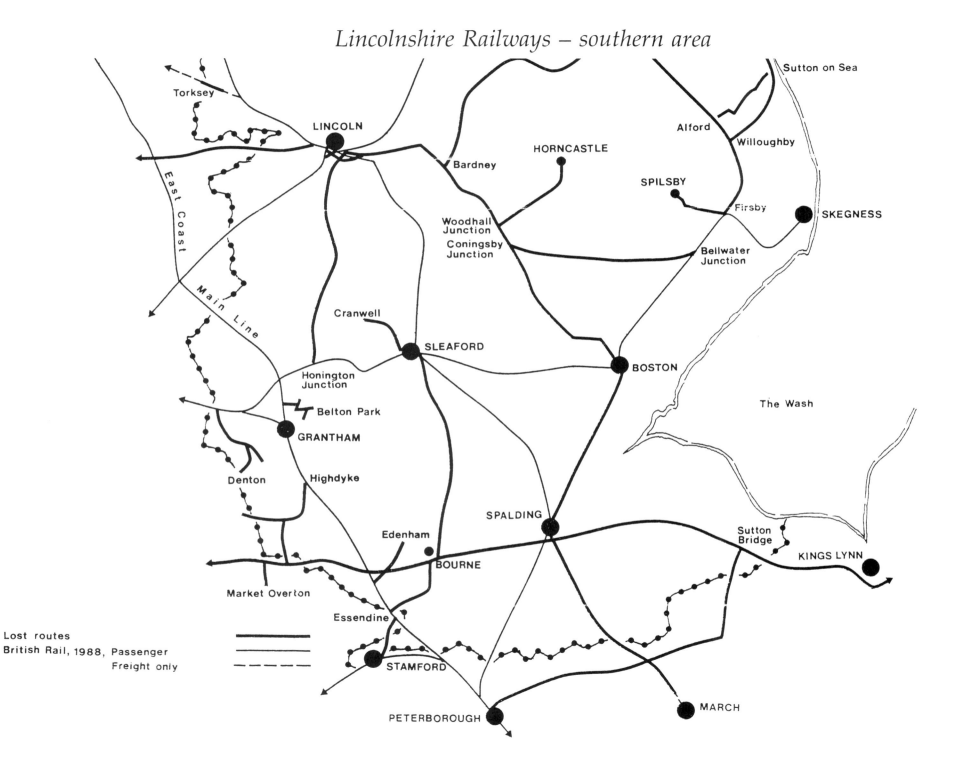

Torksey

LINCOLN

Bardney

HORNCASTLE

East Coast

Main Line

Woodhall Junction

Coningsby Junction

SPILSBY

Alford

Willoughby

Firsby

SKEGNESS

Sutton on Sea

Bellwater Junction

Cranwell

SLEAFORD

BOSTON

The Wash

Honington Junction

Belton Park

GRANTHAM

Highdyke

Denton

SPALDING

Edenham

BOURNE

Sutton Bridge

KINGS LYNN

Market Overton

Essendine

Lost routes
British Rail, 1988, Passenger
Freight only

STAMFORD

PETERBOROUGH

MARCH

The Axholme Joint Railway

This was one of the first lines in the country to be built under the 1896 Light Railways Act which permitted the construction of a railway under a Board of Trade Order, without incurring the need for heavy Parliamentary expenses. The intention was to encourage the construction of lightly laid lines with minimum earthworks along which trains ran at slow speeds. It was hoped that this would bring rail transport to sparsely populated rural areas.

The Axholme Joint was a prime example of such a line. Indeed, that built was but a proportion of what was proposed, and its emphasis on the provision of goods sidings (*see* Figure 1.1), sixteen in addition to yards at its nine passenger stations, indicates that it was always envisaged to be more important for freight than people. Blacker Siding, Whitgift Siding, Ealand Depot, Hagg Lane Siding, Hatfield Moor, Sandtoft and Burnham Lane Siding were for public use, the remainder private.

The first six miles, from Marshland Junction near Goole to Reedness, were built by the Goole and Marshland Railway and opened on 1 January 1900. A further six miles, from Reedness to a terminus at Fockerby, and four miles to Crowle opened without ceremony on 10 August 1902. The eight-mile length from Crowle to Haxey Junction was delayed by the construction of a swing bridge at Crowle (Figure 1.2), opening for goods on 14 November 1904, and for passenger trains on 2 January 1905. The final six-mile section, the goods only branch from Epworth to Hatfield Moor, opened to Allertons Siding on 5 January 1909 and Hatfield on 22 February that year. Other proposed lines, to Newlands from Epworth, and from Fockerby to Alkborough and Winteringham, crossing the River Trent by a bridge or tunnel, were never built.

Construction of the line south of Reedness was undertaken

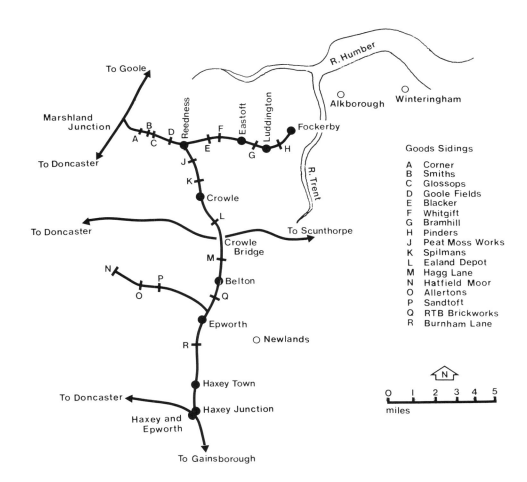

Goods Sidings

A	Corner
B	Smiths
C	Glossops
D	Goole Fields
E	Blacker
F	Whitgift
G	Bramhill
H	Pinders
J	Peat Moss Works
K	Spilmans
L	Ealand Depot
M	Hagg Lane
N	Hatfield Moor
O	Allertons
P	Sandtoft
Q	RTB Brickworks
R	Burnham Lane

Figure 1.1   *The Axholme Joint Railway*

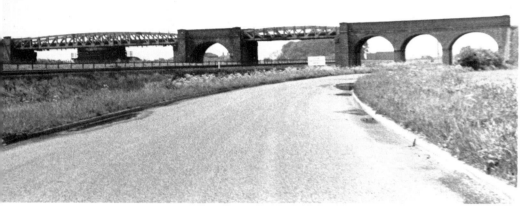

Figure 1.2 *Crowle Swing Bridge, the principal engineering feature. The viaduct and bridge together were 330 feet long. The girder bridge over the road and the Scunthorpe to Doncaster Railway was 52 feet long, the swing bridge over the Stainforth and Keadby Canal 104 feet long. The 1898 Light Railway Order required this to be normally open for the canal, and swung for trains. The pier was on the canal bank and housed the machinery although it could also be swung by hand. There was a ten mph speed limit, and at one time a signal box stood at the south end of the brick arch on the extreme left. A quarter-mile to the south stood a twelve-arch brick viaduct over the main road, and a further nine-arch viaduct over drainage dykes. The viaducts and bridges have since been demolished* © Author

by the Isle of Axholme Light Railway. From 1 October 1902 the two companies, The Isle of Axholme, and The Goole and Marshland, were acquired by the Lancashire and Yorkshire Railway, and the North Eastern Railway, who from then on operated it under the name of The Axholme Joint Railway. It was again subsequently taken over jointly by both the London Midland and Scottish, and London and North Eastern Railways.

The principal station on the line was Epworth, the birthplace of John Wesley. On the first train, 100 people travelled from the station to Goole, the departure of the train watched by another 400. The locomotive was decorated with flags and an archway was erected over the track saying 'Success to the Work'. Of the 325 tickets issued on that day, 200 were from the town. The 1910 timetable shows three daily trains each way between Haxey and Goole, with two extra on Saturdays, and two Reedness – Fockerby services daily, with one extra Saturday train from Fockerby. There was no Sunday Service. Trains were Third Class only, and this remained virtually unchanged for the twenty-eight years the trains ran. The 19½ mile journey from Haxey Junction to Goole took one hour.

Despite this level of service, passengers were still few, except for some Market Day trains. In 1926 a Sentinel Cammell steam coach was used for many of the off peak services. However, the running of the passenger trains was uneconomic, and the last regular service ran on 15 July 1933.

It was expected from the start that freight would provide the greater revenue, and this proved to be the case. First and foremost there was agriculture, the Isle of Axholme being very fertile fenland, growing mainly potatoes, carrots and peas, but peat dug from the fen between Crowle and Thorne and the Belton brickworks also created traffic for the line.

For this traffic, together with that generated by the shops and factories in the small towns and villages of the area, sixteen public delivery sidings, nine of them at the line's stations, and

Figure 1.3 *Axholme Joint Railway timetable, May 1932*
Bradshaws Guide, courtesy E Neve Collection

GOOLE, FOCKERBY, CROWLE, and HAXEY JUNCTION (One class only).—L.M.&S. and L.&N.E.

Miles.	Down.	Week Days only. mrn	mrn S		aft B	aft S	aft E	aft S
	Goole .... dep.	6 45	9 32	..	12 18	3 7	5 25	5 45
5¾	Reedness Junction .. arr.	6 57	9 44	....	12 30	3 19	5 37	5 57
—	Reedness Junction dep.	..	..	..	..	..	5 41	..
8¾	Eastoft	....	....	....	....	....	5 50	....
10	Luddington	..	..	..	..	..	5 54	..
11¼	Fockerby .... arr.	....	....	....	....	....	5 58	....
—	Reedness Junction .. dep.	6 58	9 45	..	12 32	3 20	5 39	5 59
8¾	Crowle 905, 911 .. arr.	7 6	9 53	....	12 40	3 28	5 47	6 7
	Crowle 905, 911 .. dep.	7 7	9 54	..	12 41	3 29	5 48	6 8
13	Belton	7 19	10 6	....	12 53	3 41	6 0	6 20
14¾	Epworth	7 25	10 12	..	12 59	3 47	6 6	6 26
17¾	Haxey Town	7 33	10 20	....	1 7	3 55	6 14	6 34
19½	Haxey Junc. 892, 893 ar.	7 37	10 24	..	1 11	3 59	6 18	6 38

Miles.	Up.	Week Days only. mrn	mrn S		aft B	aft S	aft E	aft S	
	Haxey Junction .... dep.	8 0	10 50	..	1 30	4 15	6 50	7 20	..
1¾	Haxey Town	8 5	10 55	....	1 35	4 20	6 55	7 25	....
4¾	Epworth	8 13	11 4	..	1 43	4 28	7 3	7 33	..
6½	Belton	8 22	11 12	....	1 50	4 35	7 10	7 40	....
10¾	Crowle 905, 911 .. arr.	8 33	11 24	..	2 1	4 46	7 21	7 51	..
	Crowle 905, 911 .. dep.	8 34	11 25	....	2 2	4 47	7 22	7 52	....
13¾	Reedness Junction .. arr.	8 42	11 33	..	2 10	4 55	7 30	8 0	..
—	Mls Fockerby ...... dep.	8E25	....	....	....	....	6 20	....	....
—	1¼ Luddington	8E29	..	..	..	..	6 24	..	..
—	2¼ Eastoft	8E33	....	....	....	....	6 28	....	....
—	5½ Reedness Junc. . arr.	8E42	..	..	..	..	6 37	..	..
—	Reedness Junction .. dep.	8 47	11 34	....	2 13	4 58	7 31	8 1	....
19½	Goole 932, 939 ..... arr.	9 0	11 47	..	2 26	5 11	7 44	8 14	..

B Weds. and Sats. **E** or E Except Sats. **S** Sats. only.

half a mile on Hatfield Moor. Forty years later the respective mileages had grown to over twelve miles and almost four miles. Both factories are still in production today, but now they use road transport.

Another narrow gauge railway associated with the line ran north and east from Hagg Lane Siding to farms on North Moor at Belton. Established after the First World War it grew to include two branches with a total of three miles. It was a horse-worked, privately owned agricultural line, taking produce to Hagg Lane Siding, and fertiliser and seed potatoes into the fields. It had disappeared by 1960, although it did survive at least until the early 1950s.

In 1950 there were three daily freight trains on the line, the traffic being mainly potatoes, celery, peas, carrots, swedes and peat moss. The beginning of the end came soon after, however, when from 1 February 1956 the line between Epworth and

Figure 1.4   *An early view of Belton Station, with a Lancashire and Yorkshire Railway 0–6–0 locomotive and passenger train. When first constructed Belton had only one platform, but a second, together with a passing loop, was built in 1907, after which this photograph was taken. Note how low the platforms were*
Courtesy Mrs A V Campion

nine private sidings were provided. Of the latter, two served Peat Works, one, Richard, Thomas and Baldwin's Brickworks at Belton, and six served farms.

Two peat works were established alongside the railway, one at Hatfield Moor, the other at Peat Moss Works Siding almost one mile south of Reedness Junction. From both of these, narrow gauge railway lines ran out onto the Moors, carrying cut peat from the workings for processing at the factory and onward transmission over the Axholme Joint Railway. By 1920 there were some 2¼ miles of line from Peat Moss Works, and

Figure 1.5   *Eastoft Station on 18 April 1965, thirteen days after the Fockerby branch closed*   © Richard Goodman

Figure 1.6 *Looking south towards the site of Spilmans Siding on 18 July 1968. Briars are beginning to grow over the rails. The countryside is typical of the line north of Belton. Substantial earthworks were necessary south of Belton all the way to Haxey Junction*   © Author

Haxey Junction closed completely, including Haxey Town and Haxey Junction Stations and Burnham Lane Public Siding. This closure was followed by that of the Hatfield Moor Branch on 30 September 1963, after an inspection resulted in condemnation of wooden underbridges, deemed not economically repairable. The remainder of the Branch was closed shortly after, from 5 April 1965.

Occasional passenger rail tours traversed the line after 1933, and the last of these was a four-car multiple unit, chartered by the North Axholme Secondary School at Crowle, which ran on 1 April 1965. This gave the local people their final opportunity to travel the route, and many took it; hundreds of others turned out to watch the train pass.

Apart from the two Haxey stations, closed previously, on

5 April the remaining stations closed, together with the Public Delivery Sidings at Blacker, Whitgift, Ealand Depot and Hagg Lane. The other sidings had all closed before this.

The rails from Goole to Belton remained until 1972, however. The Central Electricity Generating Board proposed siting a power station here at one time but this was never built. The line was retained for loads from Keadby Power Station which could not be taken by road because of restrictions caused by swing bridges at Goole and Crowle. When road improvements removed the restrictions the line was no longer needed, and the last track was lifted. So died one of the most interesting, and most rural, of Britain's light railways.

Part of the line, on the A161 between Belton and Epworth, is now a picnic site and the route from here can be walked. The stretch from Haxey to Low Burnham is a nature reserve.

Figure 1.7 *Crowle Station on 17 August 1967. At this time the line had been closed for over two years, other than for occasional loads from Keadby Power Station, carried on the line from Belton to Goole to avoid the swing bridges at Goole and Crowle. The station clock still survived and the signal was fixed to protect the station level-crossing. The curve in the track identifies the location of a former passing loop*
© Author

The North Lindsey Light Railway, Scunthorpe to Whitton

First promoted by a group of local ironmasters, the North Lindsey Light Railway was built by the Great Central Railway to open up the ironstone reserves to the north of Scunthorpe, to serve a possible site for new blast furnaces, and to be a link in the Cross Humber communication chain. The Great Central saw the potential industrial use, and were able to keep out their rivals, the Lancashire and Yorkshire Railway, who also had designs on development in the area.

Ironstone quarrying had started in the early 1880s to the north of Scunthorpe and six pits were in operation. There was a potential demand for additional blast furnaces in the town, and, again, on the north side of the town the land was available.

The first six-mile section, from its own station in Scunthorpe to West Halton, opened in September 1906. On 15 July 1907 it was extended to Winteringham, 2½ miles away. At the same time, a half-mile siding was opened down to Winteringham Haven where a small wharf was built. Both Scunthorpe and Winteringham were terminal stations, having one platform and a run round loop. Goods sidings were provided at all stations, those at Scunthorpe taking the form of exchange sidings with the Great Central Railway, to the east of the passenger station. A one road engine shed was built near to the platform.

At Winteringham Haven two chutes to discharge slag and coal into barges were built and a cargo ferry ran from here to Hull, out on a Monday and back on Wednesday. The inaugural passenger train carried 254 passengers, and the Company was encouraged to press on with the final extension of the line,

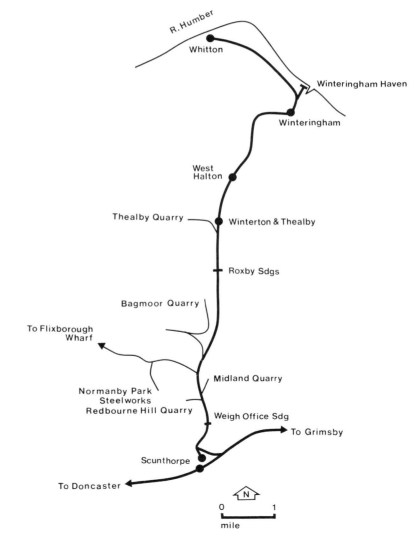

Figure 2.1   *The North Lindsey Light Railway, Scunthorpe to Whitton*

Figure 2.2   *The first train arriving at Winterton and Thealby Station, in September 1906. The engine is a Great Central Railway locomotive, typical of those used on the line*   Courtesy Scunthorpe Museum

Figure 2.3   *Winteringham Station in its early days, displaying all its period charm, from a postcard franked 20 August 1907. On the platform note the seat, nameboard, oil lamp and, unusually, a ¼-mile post*   Courtesy B Peeps

Figure 2.4   *An enlargement of part of an air photograph of Winteringham Haven, taken by the RAF in September 1946. The track layout can be seen, together with eight trucks in the siding. The trucks on the main line, to the left of the picture, were the start of a line runing all the way to Whitton*   Author's Collection

2½ miles from Winteringham, utilising part of the Haven Siding, to Whitton. For this an additional platform was built at Winteringham, giving the station one through and one terminal road, the platforms joining at their western end. At Whitton a pier was built and trains connected here with a packet sailing between Gainsborough and Hull on three days a week. It opened on 1 December 1910.

Initially, there were three passenger trains each way daily, Third Class only. One of these terminated at Winteringham, the others at Whitton. The Whitton extension was a light railway in the true sense: there were minimal facilities at the terminus, a small platform and waiting room, a run round loop with one siding, and from the beginning the level crossing gates north of Winteringham Station were opened and closed by the train crew.

Further branches from Winteringham to Barton on Humber, and Whitton to Alkborough and Burton upon Stather were proposed but because of sparse passenger traffic this idea was dropped after the First World War.

The three passenger trains had dropped to two daily trains by 1922, with no Sunday Service, and passenger trains ceased to run from 13 July 1925. It became the first major railway closure in the area this century.

In 1912 the new steelworks at Normanby Park were opened, adjacent to the line, and in the same year, on 1 August a general goods station was also opened here. Branch general goods trains usually consisted of eight or nine wagons, mostly of coal, for Winterton and Thealby, and West Halton.

There was a reorganisation of the line at its southern end

Figure 2.6　*The trackless Whitton Station prior to demolition, looking out over the River Humber. Unusually for stations on this line, the building here was on the platform. Proposals to extend the branch from here to Burton Stather, and also to the Axholme Joint Railway at Fockerby, never came to fruition*　　Courtesy Scunthorpe Museum

following the opening of a new Scunthorpe Station, to the west of the previous one, on 13 July 1925. The Light Railway Station and exchange sidings disappeared, and a new north-to-west curve was laid.

Figure 2.5　*North Lindsey Light Railway timetable, 1910. The extension to Whitton opened later that year*　　*Bradshaw's Guide,* courtesy Glenn Answer Collection

	SCUNTHORPE and WINTERINGHAM (3rd class only).—Great Central.			
Miles		Week Days.	Miles	Week Days.
		mrn aft aft		mrn aft aft
	Scunthorpe ....dep.	7 45 1 20 6 10	Winteringham ....dep.	8 20 2 0 6 37
5	Winterton and Thealby.....	8 11 36 6 23	2¼ West Halton	8 28 2 7 6 44
6	West Halton	8 4 1 39 6 26	3¼ Winterton and Thealby	8 34 2 11 6 47
8¼	Winteringham..........arr.	8 11 1 46 6 33	8¼ Scunthorpe ....arr.	8 48 2 26 7 0

Figure 2.7   Winterton and Thealby Station on 29 March 1970. Shortly after this view was taken the signal box was demolished. It was the only building actually on the platform, and being sited behind the front wall of the ticket office and waiting room, the signalman could not see trains approaching from Scunthorpe. To enable him to do so, a mirror was placed in front of it   © Glenn Answer

After the Second World War the branch was progressively pruned back. The line north of West Halton was closed on 11 October 1951, although for some years the only use beyond Winteringham had been for wagon storage. It is said that some

500 wagons lay out of use there, and they had to be moved to enable the track to be recovered. An engine and guard's van were sent to do this, the engine being coupled to the first truck. The guard then set off, returning 1½ hours later to say that he thought 500 wagons excessive, and so he had only coupled the first 265 on! The rails were removed in 1954, to be relaid at a South Yorkshire colliery.

West Halton Station was closed on 29 May 1961, and the last general goods traffic ceased with the closure on 20 July 1964 of Winterton and Thealby Station.

The southern end of the line always carried heavy ironstone traffic and over the eighty years up to 1960 quarries were opened progressively northwards to Winterton and Thealby on both sides of the line. The last new one to open was Thealby mine in 1960, and it was eventually to remove the trackbed north of Winterton.

British Rail having no further use for the line, the sole users, the British Steel Corporation, purchased the Roxby Sidings section northwards in 1967. Although British Rail retained ownership of the rest to move ore and steel products to and from the Normanby Park Steelworks, BSC engines were a daily sight over all the branch.

The last of the ironstone quarries, the Thealby Mine, closed on 23 August 1980, and the Normanby Park Works have also been closed. However, the rails to Winterton still remain in place today, very much overgrown. The southern part of the line, from Scunthorpe to the junction with the branch to Flixborough Wharf, is retained to serve the latter – a daily train takes steel products from the steelworks to the wharf for export. North of this junction it may be revived to carry household waste to fill in abandoned quarries – time alone will tell.

Figure 2.8   (On facing page) The overgrown track today, between Winterton and Thealby, and Roxby Sidings. Is this what is meant by the permanent way? © Author

New Holland Pier

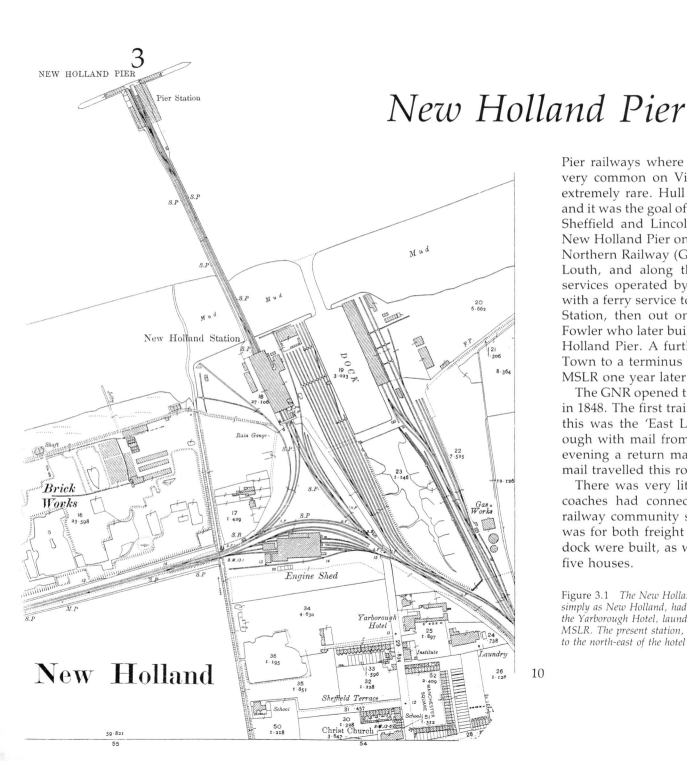

Pier railways where trains connected with boat services were very common on Victorian railways. By the 1980s they were extremely rare. Hull was once one of England's premier ports and it was the goal of the branch line opened by the Manchester, Sheffield and Lincolnshire Railway (MSLR) from Grimsby to New Holland Pier on 1 March 1848. On the same day the Great Northern Railway (GNR) opened its first line, from Grimsby to Louth, and along this then isolated length of railway joint services operated by the MSLR and the GNR ran to connect with a ferry service to Hull. The rails ran to New Holland Town Station, then out onto the 1500-foot-long pier, built by John Fowler who later built the Forth Bridge, to the terminus at New Holland Pier. A further three mile branch, from New Holland Town to a terminus at Barton on Humber, was opened by the MSLR one year later on 1 March 1849.

The GNR opened their complete line through to Peterborough in 1848. The first train of the day on the Pier arrived at 4.55 am; this was the 'East Lincolnshire Mail', arriving from Peterborough with mail from London and the eastern counties. In the evening a return mail train left the Pier at 7.43 pm. The Hull mail travelled this route until more direct routes opened later.

There was very little at New Holland before this, although coaches had connected here with ferries since 1836, and a railway community sprang up: in addition to the ferry, which was for both freight and passengers, three acres of rail-served dock were built, as well as an engine shed, a school and forty-five houses.

Figure 3.1 *The New Holland railway layout in 1906. The Town Station, then known simply as New Holland, had an overall roof. The houses north of the engine shed, the Yarborough Hotel, laundry, school, and Manchester Square, were all built by the MSLR. The present station, a simple platform and shelter, stand alongside the line to the north-east of the hotel*

10

There was also an engine shed at the Town Station, in later years an outstation of that at Immingham. In London and North Eastern Railway (LNER) days there were usually six weekday diagrams for local duties, but engines would on occasion reach Retford, Doncaster and Boston. Elderly ex-Great Central 4–4–0s predominated, and the last members of Class D7, Nos 5684 and 5704, built in 1891/2, were withdrawn from here in 1939. The shed was closed in 1941.

New Holland was regarded as the eastern terminus of the MSLR, and it was not until 1888 that through trains ceased and passengers had to change trains at Brocklesby Junction. In later years they were restored; there were two services, to Barton on Humber and to Grimsby. In 1974 the stations were served by ten Barton and ten Grimsby trains a day.

There were three tracks, a road and a footpath down the pier. The centre line was a siding used for 16 ton coal trucks carrying the fuel for the ferries. This remained until the last coal-fired ferry retired in 1978. Latterly there were two tracks, singled at the Pier Station platform, the Up line used by trains to Grimsby, the Down to Barton on Humber.

On the pier, trains were limited to 15 mph, although in LNER days drivers were instructed to reduce speed when cattle were being driven along the roadway to the boats.

The line survived the threat of closure in 1967, when goods services would have remained. The goods yard at Town Station was closed, however, in November 1979.

Whatever the future of the lines serving the area, it was obvious that the construction of the Humber Bridge would bring to an end the ferry service, and with it, trains to the Pier Station. A bridge was not a new idea. It was first mooted in 1865 by the Hull traders, as a railway bridge then, to link the port with the markets in the Midlands. The arguments raged for a hundred years, until, in March 1973 work on the longest suspension bridge in the world began.

Eight years later the bridge opened, on 24 June 1981, and the ferries ceased to run. For the last few months chalked on the buffer stop at Pier Station was the legend 'Almost the End'.

Figure 3.2   *The Pier Station in 1977. The coal trucks stabled in the centre road were a common sight, holding the fuel for the steam powered ferries. From them the coal was carried in wheelbarrows down a pontoon to the waiting boat. The layout was remodelled to give just one platform road after withdrawal of the* Lincoln Castle. *The* Farringford *can be seen on the left making its approach to the Pier*
© Tim Mawson

Figure 3.3   *New Holland Pier Station in its latter years. The run-down state of the buildings is evident. The building in the foreground is the former Pier Station signal box*
© Author

The end came on the following day, 25 June, when the Town and Pier Stations were closed after 133 years' service. The line from Brocklesby to Barton remains in use, however, and a new New Holland Station, south of the site of the Town Station, now serves the village. New Holland Pier remains in use also, for the import and export of grain and other goods, including animal feed and coal. Now, cargo boats tie up here, the remaining Pier Station buildings dwarfed by the gantries and crane of its new user. Town Station has been demolished, but three private sidings have been built at its site, on which the owners use an 0–6–0 diesel locomotive.

The dock adjacent to the Pier remained in use, and its trade has increased greatly in recent years. It handles coal, steel, scrap and fertilisers, and its owners have expansion plans. Included in these is a wish to reinstate a rail connection. The railway history of New Holland still seems secure.

Figure 3.4 *In the last week of operation a Cleethorpes train leaves New Holland Town Station*
© Author

4

The Hull to New Holland Ferry

The Humber estuary is one of the great natural barriers of the United Kingdom. It is wide and has strong tidal currents and continuously shifting sandbanks. Man has always sought to cross it by whatever means he had available, but the first regularised crossing was probably that established by the Romans from about AD 47. Over the centuries, the crossing points multiplied, and in 1803 the first service from New Holland to Hull was set up by a man called Dent, using an open boat. By 1832 a paddle-steam packet was providing three trips each way a day, and from 1836 the London Mail Coach was transferred to run to New Holland instead of Barton. In 1846 70 000 travellers used the service, although there were few buildings at New Holland and no community lived there.

It was no wonder then, that when railway companies wished to tap the resources of the Humber estuary, in particular Hull, they should seek to control what was becoming the premier ferry crossing, and in 1845 it was taken over by the Great Grimsby and Sheffield Junction Railway, later to become part of the Manchester, Sheffield and Lincolnshire Railway (MSLR). The completion of the railway and the Pier Station in 1848 ensured the future of this crossing and the demise of all the others.

Hull, Victoria Pier, to which the boats ran, was a railway station with railway staff – but no trains. The MSLR used four paddle-steamers and a horse-boat on the service initially, and in 1849 took delivery of the first of a long line of paddle-steamers ordered by the railway companies specifically for this service. The best know of these, the last three, were the *Wingfield Castle* (Figure 4.2) and the *Tattershall Castle*, built in 1934, and the *Lincoln Castle* (Figure 4.3), built in 1940.

The *Tattershall Castle* was the first to be taken out of service in 1972, after nearly forty years service in which she carried

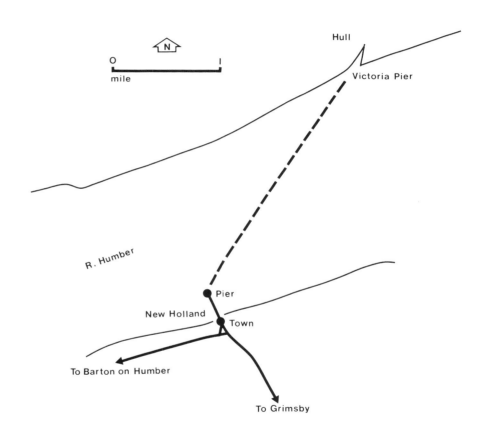

Figure 4.1 *The Hull to New Holland Ferry*

almost fifteen million passengers. In March 1974, the *Wingfield Castle* was retired and the *Lincoln Castle* became the last coal-burning paddle-steamer operating commercially in Britain. A

Figure 4.2   *The* Wingfield Castle *in mid-river trailing the usual nostalgic-smelling coal smoke behind her. She was built for the Humber crossing in 1934 by W Gray & Co at Hartlepool, together with her identical sister, the* Tattershall Castle. *She retired in March 1974 after forty years service*   Courtesy Grimsby Public Library

two-boat service was maintained, however, as Sealink transferred the *Farringford* (Figure 4.4), a diesel-electric paddle-steamer, from the Lymington to Yarmouth service on the Solent. She needed little alteration, but was changed from end-loading to side-loading for the Humber. In March 1978 the *Lincoln Castle* was withdrawn and the service became a one-boat operation until its closure on 25 June 1981. During the final weeks the boat was crowded with people taking their nostalgic last trips; the slender graceful lines of the new bridge watched over these celebrations with a superior air from the west.

In 1973 the ferries carried 750 000 people making seventeen crossings each way on a weekday and eight on a Sunday. The journey was timetabled for twenty minutes, but it could take twice as long, depending on the state of the tide and the

position of continually shifting sandbanks. The ticket (Figure 4.5) issued to pedestrians at Hull or New Holland was valid from Victoria Pier to Town Station, and included the ride, in a train, along the Pier.

To travel the route could be a dramatic experience: the paddles thudded as they ploughed the muddy brown waters; the salty breeze and the rain were often strong enough to cause passengers to climb down the steep stairway to the buffet bar;

Figure 4.3   *The* Lincoln Castle, *in mid-river, on her way to New Holland on 27 May 1974. She was a steel boat, built for the service in 1940, by the LNER at the Glasgow yard of A and J Inglis Ltd. She was also the heaviest vessel used on the service at 598 tons. After thirty-eight years she was withdrawn for repairs in February 1978. The cost of these was too great, however, and one month later it was decided not to put her back into service*   © P. Grey

and sand scraped the bottom as the steamer passed over, and occasionally, for a few seconds, was held on a bar. On the *Castles* even at the end you could wipe your feet on a LNER doormat, or pause in the passageway, lean against brass rails and watch the pistons as they turned the paddles.

On retirement the three *Castles* went off to become restaurants, the *Tattershall Castle* to London's Embankment where she is moored near Westminster Bridge, the *Wingfield Castle* first to Brighton, and later to Hartlepool, and the *Lincoln Castle* to Hessle, in the shadow of the Humber Bridge. In May 1987 the *Lincoln Castle* was moved to a new home in Alexandra Dock, Grimsby.

Figure 4.4   *The* Farringford *alongside New Holland Pier in the last week of the service before the opening of the Humber Bridge. The metal framework to the right of the photograph was the road and walkway from the Pier to a floating pontoon which gave access to the boats at all states of the tide. The pontoon was provided as one of the improvements made by the Great Central Railway in 1922*   © Author

Figure 4.5   *Ferry ticket issued 22 May 1981. The return price, £1.52, included a Victoria Pier toll and a ride on the train along the New Holland Pier, from Pier Station to Town Station*   © Author

5

Goxhill to Immingham

A railway with remarkable contrasts between attractive sleepy rural countryside on the one hand and a modern petro-chemical industrial area on the other. This six-mile line, part of the Barton and Immingham Light Railway, was opened by the Great Central Railway (GCR) in two stages, from Immingham to Killingholme on 1 December 1910 and on to Goxhill on 1 May 1911. The GCR opened its Immingham Dock in 1912 and this was one of a number of railways built to serve the dock and to encourage commercial growth in the area. A line from Ulceby to a terminus at Immingham Dock had opened for goods on 29 June 1910, and for passengers on 15 May 1912, and it was from this line that the branch diverged, half a mile west of Immingham Dock Station. There were intermediate stations on the Goxhill line at Killingholme and East Halton, but the latter having no goods sidings, was for passengers only; it also had the dubious distinction, in the First World War, of being damaged by a bomb dropped from a Zeppelin.

By 1921 another station had opened, Admiralty Platform Halt. This private halt, built originally for a small naval base, remained in use until the withdrawal of passenger trains for workers at the various riverside industries. Tickets were issued to the Halt, but there was no booking office and no tickets were issued there.

Few people lived in the area and consequently passenger traffic was low. The basic service ran from Immingham Dock to New Holland, and in the 1930s there were six trains each way on weekdays with two extra on Saturdays. There was no Sunday Service. In 1947 the weekday service had fallen to four trains each way. Further economies came; a 25 mph speed limit was introduced and both intermediate stations became Halts – request stops with no staff in attendance, East Halton on 2 August 1948, and Killingholme on 1 September 1955. The pass-

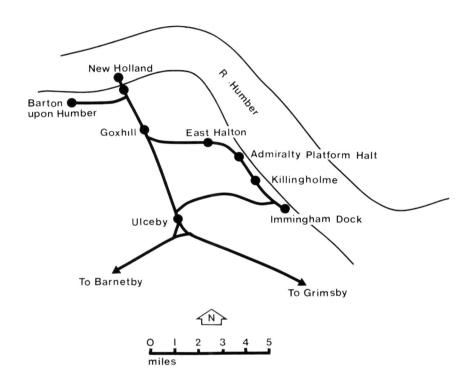

Figure 5.1 *Goxhill to Immingham*

enger service was withdrawn on 17 June 1963: East Halton closed completely and the junction at Goxhill was removed. The length from Admiralty Platform westwards was subsequently used for a short time to stable redundant trucks. Trains still ran into Immingham Dock Station from Ulceby until the passenger service was withdrawn on 6 October 1969. The line remains open for freight.

It was for freight traffic that the line was built, and the original objectives were realised. The only intermediate public delivery sidings were at Killingholme. The yard was taken over by a private company in the mid 1970s and used for the storage of steel delivered by rail but its use has now ceased. Private sidings were also provided to serve petro-chemical works, three at Admiralty Platform and one half a mile south of Killingholme.

Rail-borne traffic ceased to these works between 1970 and 1972 after the opening of the Lindsey Oil Refinery at Immingham, although two sets of sidings at Admiralty Platform remained in use up to 1983 for the storage and cleaning of rail

Figure 5.2   Killingholme Station between the wars – a single wooden platform with a simple corrugated iron booking office and waiting room. This was a remarkable contrast with the substantial brick Stationmaster's house built at the rear of the goods yard. A wagon stands in the siding to the rear of the station nameboard. The station became Killingholme Halt on 2 August 1948   Courtesy Goxhill Railway Museum

Figure 5.3   Despite its poor quality, this photograph is included because it is of particular interest. The original, stamped on the back '2? June 1912' with the station stamp, shows a Great Central Railmotor on a New Holland train at East Halton, the line having opened the previous year on 1 May 1911. East Halton was the only branch station with two platforms. The signal box in the background was removed a few years later and re-erected at Bilsthorpe Colliery, near Mansfield   Courtesy L R Durham

Figure 5.4   East Halton Station on 13 February 1974. The platforms remain with one, very overgrown, line of rails showing eleven years of disuse. There was a passing loop here, hence the two platforms. The rails have since been removed (in about 1982), but the platforms remain, together with the former station house adjacent to the road out of the picture on the left hand side   © Author

17

Figure 5.5　*The line in October 1985, looking north towards the site of Admiralty Platform Halt. This part had seen no traffic for two years although it had not been declared closed*
　　　　　　　　　　　　　　　　　　　　　　　　　　　　　　© Author

tanks. The sidings south of Killingholme Halt remain in existence although their traffic has been replaced by a pipeline.

The remnants of the line and its connections have not been declared redundant, although they are not currently used. The rails beyond a point about half a mile north of Admiralty Platform on to Goxhill were removed in about 1982 and only the platforms at East Halton remain. Admiralty Platform Halt was removed in 1975 and the station buildings at Killingholme have also gone. The truncated line with its sidings is now known as the Killingholme Branch, and it may yet be revived. The Central Electricity Board have a site for a power station adjacent to

Killingholme Station, and if it is not used for that purpose it may yet find an alternative use which will require a rail connection.

Immingham Dock is known as an important port for the import and export of a variety of commodities. What is much less known is that at one time cruise liners sailed from here also, which generated traffic on the railway and necessitated the creation of another station. After 1918 until the early 1930s 'Midnight Sun' cruises around the Norwegian Fjords and Scandinavian capital cities were very popular. A fourteen-day cruise in a 20 000 ton liner such as the *Orford, Arandora Star, Avon* or *Otranto*, cost from twenty-two guineas, and included a visit to eleven northern ports, among them Copenhagen, Oslo and Bergen. Both the Great Central and the Great Northern Railways ran special trains from London to connect with the liners, the latter routed via Peterborough, Boston, Grimsby and Ulceby. Separate trains were provided for First Class passengers, but all had dining cars and took about four hours for the trip. At Immingham the trains ran past the Dock Station onto the dockside, where the train could stop alongside the ship.

Figure 5.6　*Between the wars passengers leave the cruise ship* SS Orford *at Immingham after a Norwegian cruise. The coaching stock is labelled 'For Norway Cruises Orient Line Special', and the train is so long that the engine has run out into the River Humber along the Western Jetty protecting the lock entrance*
　　　　　　　　　　　　　　　　　　　　　　　　　Courtesy H Answer

6

The Grimsby and Immingham Tramway

The Great Central Railway chose the site at Immingham for their new deep water dock at the point where the deep-water channel of the Humber came closest to the shore. They were left with one problem, the lack of a nearby settlement for dock workers to live in and for visiting ships' crews to visit. The nearest established town, already an important port, was Grimsby, and so it was logical to build a railway between Grimsby and Immingham to provide the necessary service – and certainly cheaper than building a new town. The Grimsby and Immingham Tramway was the solution to the problem.

In 1910, two years before the dock opened, the Grimsby District Light Railway was built between the two towns. This terminated at the western end of Grimsby, in the dock area, and was not convenient for passengers from many of the housing areas and the town centre, and so a new line, part street tramway, part railway line, on which tramcars would run, was the obvious solution. The six-mile line was opened, for most of its length parallel to the Light Railway, on 15 May 1912.

The eastern terminus was at Corporation Road in Grimsby. The line ran through the streets with stops at Yarborough Street, Shortford Street and Cleveland Bridge, on to Immingham Town. There were, in addition, request stops at Jackson Street, Boulevard Recreation Ground and Cleveland Street in Grimsby, and at Great Coates Level Crossing, Number 5 Passing Place, Marsh Road Level Crossing and Kiln Lane, Stallingborough, in the open country. On 17 November 1913 a one-mile extension onto the Immingham Dock Estate was opened with a reversal at the Town Station. The depot was near West Marsh Sidings in Grimsby. It was hoped that a connection would be made with the Grimsby street tramways but this did not come to fruition because a rebuilding of Corporation Bridge prevented

it. Number 5 Passing Place was one of eight passing loops provided along the single line, at regular intervals, and numbered 1 to 8.

To operate the service, the Great Central built sixteen cars, four of these to a different specification intended to work on the street tramway system. At a later date, three tramcars were bought from the Newcastle Tramway to replace the latter. In 1951 another seventeen were purchased from the Gateshead

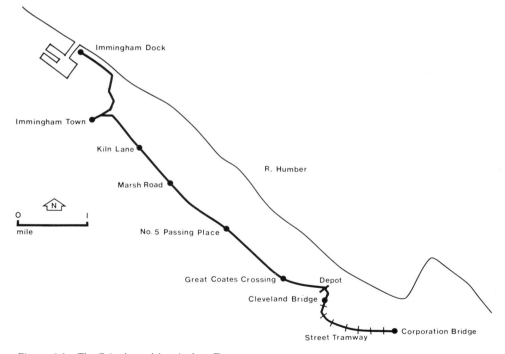

Figure 6.1 *The Grimsby and Immingham Tramway*

19

Figure 6.2 *Trams lined up at the depot in 1961. Numbers 1 and 14, both ex-Great Central cars, are 'centre stage'* © Richard Goodman

From 1 July 1956 the eastern end was truncated with the closure from Cleveland Bridge to Corporation Bridge, and complete closure came on 1 July 1961: the trams required replacement after almost fifty years' service and it was considered that a bus service would be more economic. But, in the eyes of many users it was considered a retrograde step, as

Figure 6.3 *One of the seventeen Gateshead trams converted for use on the Grimsby and Immingham Tramway. This view clearly shows the large double doors built into the side replacing the space formerly taken up by two windows* © Richard Goodman

Tramway. All single deck, the cars were of typical tramway design, with conductors to pick up the current from overhead wires, and seat backs that could be swivelled, enabling passengers to face either way.

The nature of dock work required an intensive, round-the-clock service. For example, in 1938 trams ran from 12.20 am to 11.30 pm; forty-two were time-tabled each way daily, with fourteen each way on Sundays, and at peak times, such as when shifts changed, up to six cars would run the 27-minute journey in convoy. The motion and noise of the trams when travelling at speed was notorious, earning them the local name of 'Rattlesnakes'.

At least two of the cars still survive and working – both ex-Gateshead cars, restored to their former livery. No 10 is at the North of England Open Air Museum at Beamish, and No 20 at the Crich Tramway Museum.

Few remains of the line are to be found, but a visit to Immingham will reveal a line of concrete poles, some still with pulleys attached, which carried the overhead wire, alongside the road to the eastern dock entry gates.

Figure 6.4   Car number 15 at Grimsby Corporation Bridge in 1948. The Tramway Station nameboard can be seen partly hidden behind the right hand side of the car. This was yet another unique feature, a similar board being displayed at Immingham Dock. This vehicle was the only survivor of a mishap involving numbers 2, 10 and 15 in fog, as a result of which 2 and 10 were taken out of service

Courtesy M White Collection

even in winter, when snow blocked the roads, the trams never stopped running.

The closure did not go unrecorded. Invited guests travelled on a convoy of five cars, the leader, No 4, bearing an inscription, 'Grimsby-Immingham Electric Railway, Last Day, July 1st 1961', and suitably decorated for the occasion. A celebration lunch was taken at Immingham before the return journey, the last of regular service.

Figure 6.5   Cars numbers 15 and 21 waiting at the Immingham terminus in 1961, shortly before closure of the line. For British Railways this line had many unique features, not least the vehicles themselves. This photograph enables comparison to be made between numbers 15, an ex-Great Central tram, and 21, a former Gateshead vehicle. In addition to the visible design differences, the Great Central trams had two trolley poles, one for each direction, and three compartments, a small central one being for luggage and parcels. The Gateshead trams had one trolley pole and two compartments

Courtesy Grimsby Public Library

7

The Misson Branch – Bawtry to Haxey and Epworth

The Misson Branch, as it became known, is a line about which little appears to have been written, and few records seem to have been kept. Parts of its history are shrouded in mystery.

In 1901 the Tickhill Light Railway was authorised; it was to tap the South Yorkshire Coalfield from a junction at Tickhill with the South Yorkshire Joint Railway, crossing the East Coast Main Line at Bawtry, to a junction with the Great Northern and Great Eastern Joint Line at Haxey, where coal had been discovered, and a mine was proposed. In the event, the Great Northern Railway, who eventually built it, terminated the line at Bawtry. It never reached Tickhill, the Haxey Colliery was never built, and the line never became a coal carrier. This doomed it to a tranquil existence, with one intermediate station, at Misson, for goods only, and no passenger service.

The eight miles of single track were opened on 12 August 1912. There was agricultural traffic from Misson Goods Depot, where there was also a private siding for Yorkshire Amalgamated Products, and sand and gravel from three private sidings. Two of these for Edward's and Cullen's quarries, were at the Bawtry end, the other for William Oates, half a mile west of Misson.

This traffic kept the western end, the 2¾ miles to Misson, open but the remainder had succumbed at an unknown date prior to 1923. A ¾-mile stretch, two miles east of Misson was removed, and one theory is that it was taken to France in World War One, although there is no conclusive evidence for this. The truncated length from Haxey and Epworth was retained and used for many years for wagon storage, but with no maintenance the track was in a parlous state, and when in 1950 a

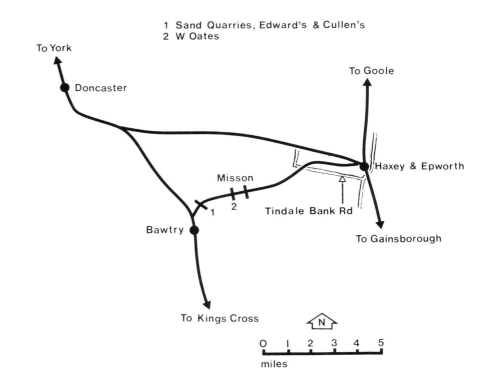

Figure 7.1 *The Misson Branch – Bawtry to Haxey and Epworth*

Director 4–4–0 ventured onto the branch to shunt wagons the track burst apart beneath it, leading to complete closure of the eastern end. The western end, however, carried on.

In the days of the London and North Eastern Railway (LNER) there was a 25 mph speed limit, which by 1960 had fallen to 15 mph. Only Misson level-crossing had gates, the others did not, and drivers were instructed to slow to 10 mph and be ready to stop if necessary at them.

Because Misson Depot consisted only of a loop, trains having worked from Bawtry with the engine in front, reversed on return with the brake van leading.

In the latter years of the LNER the traffic in sand and agricultural produce justified two return trips daily. Twenty years later the train ran 'as required' and very infrequently at that. December 7 1964 saw the final closure of this unusual line.

Figure 7.2   *There were few earthworks on the line. An embankment leading to a bridge over Tindale Bank Road was constructed on the section latterly used for wagon storage from Haxey and Epworth Station. The bridge has now gone, as has the embankment to the right of the road, but the abutment remains. The length of line south from here is a very good example of how the area's farmers have reclaimed many lengths of line, incorporating them into adjacent fields*   © Author

8

The Leverton Branch – Cottam to Torksey

The main routes of the Manchester, Sheffield and Lincolnshire Railway (MSLR) ran east–west, and they opened their Retford-to-Gainsborough line in July 1849. In the same year the Great Northern Railway (GNR) opened their line between Lincoln and Gainsborough. The MSLR, later the Great Central, wanted to reach Lincoln, and in the following year, on 7 August 1850, they opened their Leverton Branch, from Clarborough Junction on their Gainsborough line to Sykes Junction with the GNR, eight miles north-west of Lincoln.

The line was double-track, eight miles long, with stations at Leverton, Cottam and Torksey. The one great engineering feature was the Torksey Viaduct over the River Trent. A steel girder bridge, with stone abutments, 320 feet long, over the

river, approached from Torksey by a steel trestle viaduct 530 feet long. The Company had running powers over the GNR to Lincoln Central Station and they established a goods yard and engine shed in the city.

The 1938 timetable shows fourteen passenger trains each way daily between Lincoln and Sheffield, and one each way Retford/Lincoln. Four of these did not stop at the line's three stations, another stopped at Torksey only and one Sheffield/Lincoln train called at Leverton only.

For many years, up to its closure, the Leverton line was the route taken by the fishermen's excursion trains which ran on Saturdays and Sundays from Sheffield and Rotherham, to the stations on the Lincolnshire Loop Line between Lincoln and

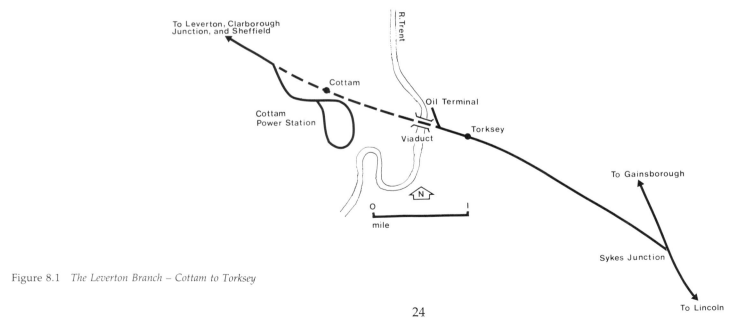

Figure 8.1 *The Leverton Branch – Cottam to Torksey*

24

Figure 8.2 *Torksey Station in 1961. When the Leverton Branch was closed in 1959, the route aquired the function of so many redundant routes, that of wagon storage. This part reopened in 1966 as a private siding serving Torksey Oil Depot. The line was singled, and the station buildings were demolished, in 1967* © Richard Goodman

Boston. There could be two fishermen's trains a day on Summer Saturdays, as well as coast excursion traffic from Yorkshire to Lincolnshire's seaside resorts.

The route was closed on 2 November 1959, and the stations lost their goods and passenger services.

Subsequently, however, there was a renaissance of freight traffic. An oil terminal had been established during the Second World War adjacent to the River Trent at Torksey, to which deliveries were made from a river wharf. The depot became rail-served from 31 January 1966 with the construction of two sidings alongside the river from the branch. The 2¾-mile line from Sykes Junction operated as a private siding, with two sets of level-crossing gates being operated by the train crew. The depot was visited on a daily basis, Tuesday to Friday, by an oil tanker train from Ellesmere Port. The depot closed at the end of June 1988, and unless taken over by another rail user it seems destined to become a further lost Lincolnshire line.

In 1968 a coal-fired power station opened at Cottam, on the west bank of the river. The line from Clarborough Junction was reinstated and is used by 'merry-go-round' coal trains from the Nottinghamshire Coalfield. A short length of line, 1½ miles long, including the Torksey Bridge and Cottam Station, is disused, and the rails have been removed.

Figure 8.3 *The Torksey Viaduct and Bridge, over the broad River Trent, in 1984*
© Author

9

The East Lincolnshire Main Line

The East Lincolnshire Main Line was the first route opened by the Great Northern Railway (GNR). Although one section remained open, and another was subsequently reopened after its initial closure, it is important, as far as its history is concerned, to consider the whole line in detail.

The first fourteen miles, from Louth to Grimsby, opened on 1 March 1848, and the first trains ran through to the Humber Ferry at New Holland, over the line opened by the Manchester, Sheffield and Lincolnshire Railway (MSLR), from Grimsby, on the same day. In September 1847 a special train had run to Grimsby from Louth with invited guests. At Louth, thousands turned out to witness this event, regarded as the wonder of the age by the local populace. A regular service, of five trains each way on weekdays, and two on Sundays was introduced, taking fifty-two minutes for the journey, and stopping at the intermediate stations, Waltham, Holton le Clay, North Thoresby and Ludborough.

On 3 September 1848 the next eighteen miles from Louth to Firsby were opened, together with stations at Legbourne Road, Authorpe, Aby, Alford Town, Willoughby, Burgh le Marsh and Firsby. The line to Boston, with intermediate stations at Little Steeping, Eastville, Old Leake and Sibsey, opened on 1 October 1848, and the line on to Werrington Junction, north of Peterborough, sixteen days later, with stations at Kirton, Algarkirk and Sutterton, Surfleet, Spalding, Littleworth, St James Deeping and Peakirk.

With double track throughout and three of the larger stations – Louth, Alford Town and Firsby – roofed overall, for the next 122 years the East Lincolnshire provided a speedy, efficient route to and from the capital, with initially main-line and subsequently secondary main-line status.

At first five daily trains still ran through to New Holland from

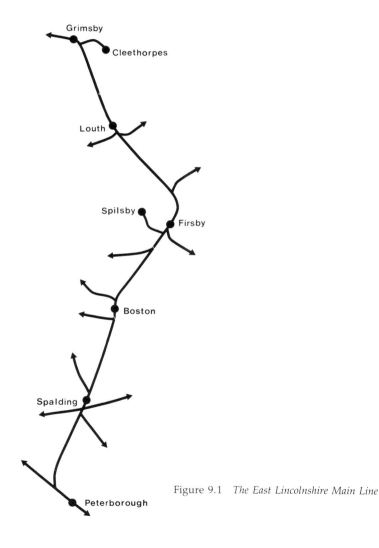

Figure 9.1 *The East Lincolnshire Main Line*

Figure 9.1(a)   *The East Lincolnshire Main Line – northern end*   Figure 9.1(b)   *The East Lincolnshire Main Line – southern end*

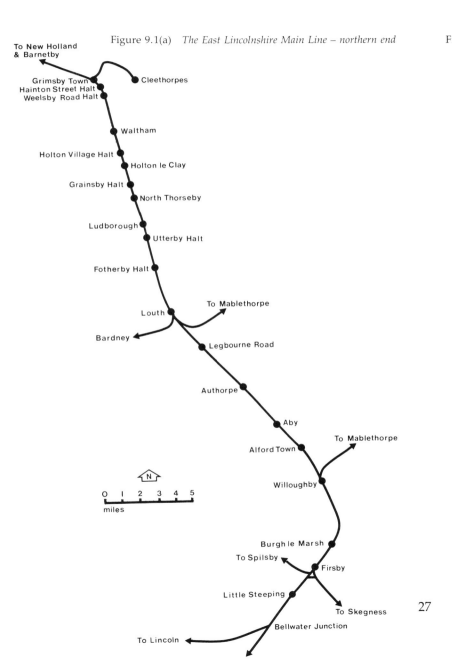

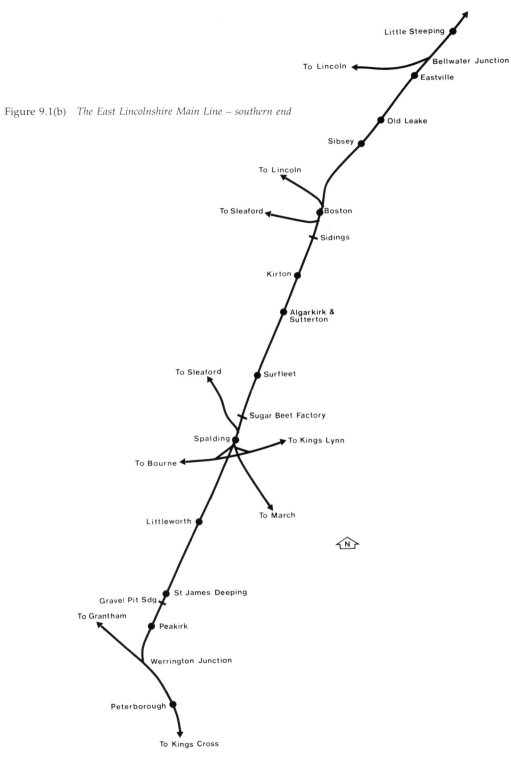

27

Figure 9.2 *A delightful period photograph of Alford Town Station in GNR days. It then had its overall roof, and a southbound train, complete with a GNR 2–2–2 locomotive, is the star attraction* Courtesy P Grey Collection

Peterborough. The most interesting was the 'East Lincolnshire Mail'. Worked by the Eastern Counties Railway to Peterborough and there handed over to the GNR, it departed at 1.43 am, and, calling at principal stations, reached New Holland at 4.55 am. The southbound mail left New holland at 7.43 pm, arriving at Peterborough at 10.48 pm. There were two trains each way between Louth and New Holland. On Sundays there was only one through-train in each direction plus the mail trains. Fares from London were

	First Class	Second Class	Third Class
Boston	18s 10d	14s 2d	8s 11d
New Holland	£1 10s 1d	£1 2s 7d	14s 3d
Hull	£1 10s 7d	£1 2s 11d	14s 7d

By 1890 there were six weekday trains from Peterborough to New Holland, and one to Grimsby only. On Wednesdays there were two additional Louth/Grimsby return journeys. Very little change occurred over succeeding years other than that trains eventually began or terminated at Grimsby.

Through trains from Grimsby to London and return began in the early years of this century. Before this Grimsby passengers could use the 2.0 pm Manchester express from Kings Cross, which slipped a carriage at Retford for Grimsby. In 1914 through-trains from Grimsby left at 6.0 am, 9.15 am, and 12.35 pm, with just one through-return leaving the Capital at 4.0 pm. In 1938 through-trains left at 9.20 am and 12.45 pm, with a 4.5 pm return.

For many years the first morning train from Grimsby departed southwards around 6.0 am. This connected at Peterborough with the 8.30 am London express from Grantham, which, on Mondays, was used by county Corn Merchants visiting the London market. In the mid 1930s a Grimsby-to-Peterborough express was provided; leaving Grimsby at 7.15 am, and calling only at Louth, Firsby, Boston and Spalding, it arrived in Peterborough to connect with a 9.10 am London express. This arrived at Kings Cross at 10.28 am. Grimsby travellers were in the City in under 3¼ hours, which was about half an hour quicker than the next best time. The return service connected at Peterborough with the 7.25 pm Kings Cross–Leeds express. Leaving at 8.42 pm, with the same calls as in the morning, it reached Grimsby at 10.29 pm. This train included a buffet car, and, probably because it was the fastest on the line, it became known locally as 'The Flying Flea'.

Figure 9.3 *GNR Stirling 8-ft Single No 1004. This was used on expresses between Peterborough, Boston and Grimsby in 1905 to 1912*

Courtesy E Neve Collection

The first locomotives used on the East Lincolnshire Main Line were the Sharp 2–2–2 Singles, followed around 1870 by Sturrock 2–2–2 and 2–4–0 engines. Later, when the Stirling 2–2–2 and 4–2–2 8-foot Singles were displaced from main-line duties around the turn of the century, they were transferred to the county and worked out their last years here on secondary duties. In their turn they were replaced by Ivatt small Atlantics, the 'Klondykes', and their larger sisters until replaced first by the Thompson B1 4–6–0s at the end of the Second World War. From 1959 Britannia Pacifics displaced from East Anglia by dieselisation were also used.

Equally important to the development of the East Lincolnshire Main Line was its freight traffic, particularly carrying fish, potatoes and sugar beet. The MSLR and the GNR both opened their first lines into Grimsby in 1848. At that time there was a small dock in the town, opened in 1800, but it was in decline; there was no fishing industry, and the population of the town was falling. Acting co-operatively the two railway companies were to transform this situation, and by 1881 Grimsby had become the premier fishing port in the United Kingdom.

The first fishing smack landed its catch here in 1850, and the GNR, seeing an opportunity, encouraged a fleet of thirteen smacks to relocate here from Manningtree in Essex. In 1854 the two railway companies sponsored the formation of the Grimsby Deep Sea Fishing Company, and in 1856 fourteen smacks moved to Grimsby from London and Brixham. At first they used the cargo dock, but a separate fish dock and market was opened in 1856. It was extended in 1860, and followed by No 2 fish dock in 1870, itself extended in 1900. Rail traffic in fish grew from 500 tons in 1852, to 3400 tons in 1857, 10 360 tons in 1865, and 26 234 tons in 1870. By 1881 Grimsby landed one

Figure 9.4 *LNER Class D3 4–4–0 No 4352 on a trial trip from Doncaster Works after an overhaul. This type was used extensively on the East Lincolnshire line and its branches*

Courtesy E Neve Collection

Figure 9.5 *Wragby Junction signal box, half a mile south of Louth Station, in about 1920. The tall box was reduced in height in 1922. The southbound express has an LNER Class D9 4–4–0 at its head, an ex-Great Central locomotive*
Courtesy P Grey Collection

third of all the fish for England and Wales. In the early years the GNR was the main beneficiary, as fish was regarded as a luxury food and its main market was London. In later years demand grew in the industrial north of England, and the MSLR, later the Great Central, reaped its benefit. For many years two express fish trains ran every night from Grimsby to Kings Cross.

The coming of the railway also caused the rapid expansion of the commercial docks at Grimsby. Much of the credit for this goes to the MSLR, who developed their own shipping services to the Continent, exporting coal and importing raw materials to serve industries in the north of England already served by their own lines.

The Lincolnshire soil is extremely fertile, and one of its main crops has always been potatoes, for which the Fenland soils in the Boston and Spalding areas are particularly suitable. The chief difficulty in the early days was getting them to market: grown in fields surrounding the many small villages and hamlets, they were a bulky crop and difficult to transport.

Ever eager to develop traffic, the GNR offered special concessions to growers, giving generous allowances to cover the cost of cartage to the nearest railway station. Given access by rail to markets nationwide, the industry rapidly expanded and potatoes assumed great importance at all the stations on lines radiating from Spalding and Boston, and especially, among the smaller stations on the line, particularly Littleworth and Kirton.

The principal potato-growing farming company was Messrs Dennis and Sons, farming in all some 7000 acres. Of these about 2000 acres each were in the neighbourhood of Littleworth and Kirton Stations. At Kirton, in the station yard, they built their own warehouse, and at Littleworth, they had their own

Figure 9.6 *Ivatt Atlantic, 4–4–2 No 4403, with a southbound express passing Neaversons Siding, Peakirk, in 1934*   Courtesy E. Neve

Figure 9.7 *Cleethorpes – Kings Cross express passing Peakirk in August 1938. The engine is a rebuilt 4–4–2, No 3279* © E Neve

network of eleven route-miles of two-foot narrow-gauge railway. This terminated on a loading dock north of Littleworth Station from where potatoes were transferred direct into stand-ard-gauge trucks. Built during the First World War, it was oper-ated until 1950. Wagons laden with potatoes were collected from the wayside stations by the local goods trains and taken into either Boston or Spalding.

The harvesting of potatoes began in July of each year, and in the summer months between the wars the traffic was so heavy that the six or seven normal daily trains would be doubled, or even trebled. Two to four hundred wagon-loads were despatched daily for six months of the year. Destinations were countrywide, and to Hull, Liverpool, London and Southampton docks for export. Train loads of seed potatoes, mainly from Scotland, were a major import by rail into the area.

Also in the years between the wars sugar beet became an important railborne product. In 1926 a branch line, one mile long, was opened from a point one mile north of Spalding Station to the newly opened sugar beet factory, one of a number built around this time in eastern England. Beet wagons were worked from most country stations to their local factory, and coal in, and finished products out, generated additional revenue.

Other private sidings served gravel workings south of St James Deeping Station and a woodyard just over a mile south of Boston Station.

Locomotive depots were built at Grimsby, Louth, Boston and Spalding. Only one of these was on the now closed section, that at Louth. Its engines worked the main line as well as the branches to Bardney, and to Willoughby via Mablethorpe. In British Railways days its shedcode was 40C, and it closed in 1956.

Figure 9.8 *On June 4 1940 a northbound train with an Ivatt 4–4–2 at its head approaches Louth. The photograph was taken from the Monks Dyke level-crossing and the train is passing over the Bardney Line junction* © B Stephenson

Figure 9.9 *A LNER steam railcar at North Thoresby. The external coal-bunker on the forward end of the vehicle indicates that this was one of the eleven supplied to the LNER after 1927, built by Clayton Wagons Ltd of Lincoln. Number 2122, Railway, was, like the others, named after former horse-drawn mail-coaches. Seating sixty-four people in great comfort, they were at first cheap to operate. This one, worked from Grimsby for a short time prior to being transferred to Annesley in July 1929*
Courtesy J Hickling

In 1886, on the opening of the Sutton and Willoughby Railway, a new station was provided at Willoughby, north of the level-crossing, to serve branch and main line trains. The station it replaced was to the south of the level-crossing.

In an effort to stimulate additional passenger traffic at the northern end of the line, on 11 December 1905, the GNR introduced a steam-railcar service between Grimsby and Louth and opened Halts at Fotherby, Utterby, Grainsby, Holton Village, and at Weelsby Road and Hainton Street in Grimsby. The platforms were short and low, built of wood and rubble filled. They were unstaffed and tickets were issued on the train by Conductor Guards. No goods sidings were provided. Six railcars were built but they were not a success as extra carriages could not be added to cope with peak demands. The experiment was short-lived, the railcars being replaced by a locomotive-hauled four-coach set.

During the Second World War, between 1940 and 1943, the line was the haunt of one of a number of armoured trains stationed on the south and east coasts to provide mobile support for the Army in the event of an invasion. First based in July 1940 at Louth, and from the following September in Grimsby, it patrolled between Boston and Grimsby, venturing also to New Holland, on the Mablethorpe Loop, and to Skegness. In 1941 it was moved to Spalding to work the routes radiating from there, visiting Boston, Sleaford, Bourne, Peterborough, March and Sutton Bridge. From February 1942 to 1943 it was based at Boston and resumed patrols to Grimsby. These armoured trains consisted of a tank engine, a spare tender

Figure 9.10 *Utterby Halt, opened in December 1905, with a southbound GNR steam rail-motor at the diminutive platform* Courtesy Great Northern Railway Society

carrying extra supplies of coal and water, two open wagons and two armoured trucks with six-pounder guns. They were also equipped with anti-tank guns, machine guns and small arms, and crewed by thirty soldiers. In the event, their main success was visiting local towns in connection with the National Savings campaign, 'War Weapons Week'!

In February 1947, the winter of the 'big freeze' when, for a time, a cattle train was marooned between Legbourne Road and Authorpe, an interesting experiment was carried out in Lincolnshire. The Ministry of Supply wanted to evaluate the use of twin-mounted jet engines to remove snow. The exercise was carried out in the Louth area, the engines mounted on a truck propelled by a locomotive. They melted the snow but it

Figure 9.11   The Railway Correspondence and Travel Society Lincolnshire Rail Tour at Louth on 16 May 1954, with Gresley J6 0–6–0, No 64199   © R K McKenny

Figure 9.12   Louth Station in 1967. The beautiful Tudor Gothic proportions of the building are self-evident, with the ornate arcaded porte-cochère *over the main entrance. The principal stations on the line, at Alford, Burgh le Marsh and Firsby, also had this embellishment, but none were so fine as this. The function was to give a sense of occasion to travel by train and to indicate the importance of the station. It also kept those who arrived by horse and carriage dry*   © Author

was found difficult to remove packed ice without damage to the permanent way. The experiment was also carried out on roads in the area, removing much of the road surface in the process. Needless to say, the idea never caught on!

Before the 1960s station closures were sporadic. Passenger trains ceased to call at Grainsby Halt in 1939, Weelsby Road Halt in 1940, Legbourne Road in 1953, Holton le Clay in 1955 and Old Leake in 1956. But the 1960s were traumatic times. The 11 September 1961 was a sad day for Lincolnshire's railways, the day on which twenty-five intermediate rural stations

Figure 9.13   *A typical country station scene in the interwar period. This is Aby, in the 1930s. There are eleven wagons in the sidings, and initials on some denote their origin. In addition to local ones there are visitors from the London Midland and Scottish, and the Great Western Railways, aptly illustrating the importance of the railway in the national economy. Aby had staggered platforms: the station house stands on the down platform, the up being past the signal box, on the other side of the level-crossing*
Courtesy P Carter

Figure 9.14   *Authorpe Station on 28 April 1972. The removal of track is under way and the line has been singled from here northwards. This was another example of staggered platforms, the up platform was on the other side of the level-crossing*
© Author

countywide lost their passenger services. Seventeen* of these were on this line, although the remaining East Lincolnshire stations, at Firsby, Burgh le Marsh, Willoughby, Alford Town, Louth and North Thoresby, retained theirs until final closure. The same day saw the first goods yard closure, at Aby.

The first proposal to close down the route came in 1963; the only result, however, was that North Thoresby and Surfleet lost their freight services. But 1964 was a successful year for the merchants of doom, and fifteen goods yards were closed. Three more yards were closed in 1966, and from then freight was handled only at Grimsby, Louth, Boston and Spalding.

Another successful fight against total closure came in 1966, but it served only to stave off the day of reckoning, which came on 5 October 1970, when trains ceased to run from Grimsby to Peterborough, and the area lost its two direct trains each way daily to London, together with six connections each way at Peterborough.

The last passenger trains ran on Saturday 3 October 1970, extra coaches being added to the normal trains. At Grimsby, the Station Manager was in mourning, at Louth 200 people waved, and at Alford Town a band played the Last Post. A special Grimsby–London train, arranged by the Lincolnshire Standard Group of Newspapers, calling at the intermediate stations, gave the local people the opportunity for a day in London, and the last up through-train was powered by Class 47, No 1577. North Thoresby, Louth, Alford Town, Willoughby, Burgh le Marsh, and Firsby Stations then closed. About a hundred British Rail staff were affected but in the event only twenty of these, mainly level-crossing keepers, were made redundant.

All was not lost, however. The line between Boston and Firsby South Junction was retained as part of the link between Skegness and the Midlands, a role it still serves, and freight

* Hainton Street Halt, Waltham, Holton Village Halt, Ludborough, Utterby Halt, Fotherby Halt, Authorpe, Aby, Little Steeping, Eastville, Sibsey, Kirton, Algarkirk and Sutterton, Surfleet, Littleworth, St James Deeping and Peakirk

the years this link increased in importance and the level of service rose, and when the line from Spalding to March closed in 1982, all services were diverted into Peterborough. The future of the line now seems secure.

The rails from Louth to Grimsby, the original length, were singled and retained for the bulk-shipment of grain from Associated British Maltsters Ltd at Louth to destinations at home and abroad. This traffic kept the line busy for another ten years, but then ceased, the line closing on 28 December 1980, after 132 years. Traffic to Spalding Sugar Beet Factory ceased in 1980 and that short length was then closed.

In 1978 the Grimsby–Louth Rail Group was formed to

Figure 9.15 *Hainton Street Halt in August 1961, a month before it was closed. This was one of the halts introduced in 1905 to stimulate passenger traffic on the northern end of the line. The signal cabin, which pre-dated it, controlled the level-crossing. The simple construction of these halts is visible, low, short platforms with, on one, an open-fronted wooden shelter. This is one of the sites being utilised by the Grimsby – Louth Railway Preservation Society. The signal cabin has been restored and railway materials are stored where the platforms and track once stood. Trains may run here again one day*   Courtesy Grimsby Public Library

trains still ran from Grimsby to Louth, and from Spalding to the sugar beet factory.

On 7 June 1971 a remarkable renaissance took place. Spalding Station had remained open, as it was on the Great Northern and Great Eastern route from Doncaster to March. The townspeople were not happy with their services to London and after the local councils agreed to subsidise it, the line from there to Peterborough reopened, with one train a day each way. Over

Figure 9.16 *The last weekend that trains ran, and a railcar passes the site of Kirton Station. Kirton lost its passenger trains on 11 September 1961, and its goods yard closed on 15 June 1964*   © P. Grey

on Saturday 20 December 1980, organised two return-trips over the route, carrying 125 passengers and Father Christmas, who gave presents to the children. People came mainly from the

Figure 9.17   *The goods shed and yard at Firsby in July 1971. Many stations serving market towns, or which were important junctions, were provided with a roof covering both platforms and the space in between. Louth and Alford had them, but most had gone by the early 1950s. Firsby retained its cover to the end, even though the central section of the roof-covering above the track had been removed some time before. An indication of attention to detail of design is given by the wrought iron spandrels on top of the columns which supported the centre of the roof*   © Author

Figure 9.18   *Willoughby Station, one month after the line closed. The signals have already been removed. The platform on the left was an island, the Mablethorpe trains using the other face. This station was opened in 1888, with the line to Sutton on Sea, as a junction station. It replaced an earlier one, built forty years before, which stood on the other side of the level-crossing. The graceful iron footbridge survives at a fishing lake near Burgh le Marsh*   © Author

campaign for the reintroduction of a passenger service on the freight line. It was subsequently re-formed as the Grimsby–Louth Railway Preservation Society, on the announcement by British Rail of their decision to close it. Their intention was (and is) to restore a railway service along the route. It was they who, expected to be the base initially and track will at an early stage be laid to Louth so that income can be gained from tourism. The long term intention is again to link Louth and Grimsby.

Finally, a poignant note – Alford Town Station and goods yard are now an industrial estate. The road serving it is named Beeching Way. Very appropriate!

Figure 9.19   The A16 level-crossing in Spalding in 1985. This last remnant of part of the East Lincolnshire Main Line was singled after most of the route closed in 1970, and used until 1980 to give access to the Sugar Beet Factory sidings
© Author

Figure 9.20   Class 08 diesel shunter, then numbered 3554, at Alford Town with the demolition train on 28 April 1972. The station and yard are now an industrial estate, the road serving it aptly named Beeching Way   © Author

locality, but some had travelled from London and Plymouth in an effort to support this special trip.

Although the track has now gone, the Preservation Society have applied for a Light Railway Order, and are negotiating for purchase of the trackbed. They have occupied Haven Street Crossing (in Grimsby) and Louth North signal boxes, and have restored them to their original condition. The latter is the last of the five boxes that once controlled Louth's trains. Two 1957 0–4–0 Fowler engines have been donated by Conoco, and the Society also have a few items of rolling stock. Ludborough is

10

The Mablethorpe Branches

From minor agricultural beginnings the railway became the direct cause of the development of the holiday industry to Mablethorpe and Sutton on Sea, and, later, literally a lifeline to a drowning town. The area has much to thank its erstwhile railways for.

Mablethorpe was first connected to the outside world by the

Louth and East Coast Railway, which opened its single line of ten miles of rails on 17 October 1877. It was built primarily for agricultural traffic, and had small stations at Grimoldby, Saltfleetby and Theddlethorpe, each with a single platform for passengers and one or two sidings – Saltfleetby had two, the others, one each. It had an inauspicious birth – the first train, travelling backwards, crashed through two sets of level-crossing gates! Nevertheless a service of seven trains each way, with one on Sundays, was introduced.

Figure 10.2 *Grimoldby's well-kept station between the wars*

Courtesy J E Hurton

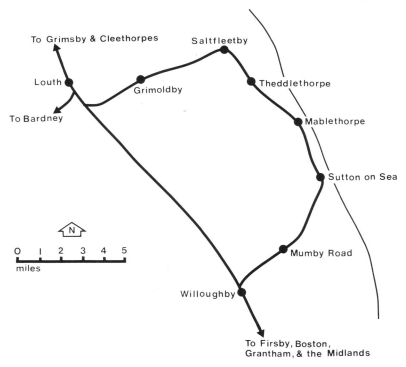

Figure 10.1 *The Mablethorpe Branches*

Figure 10.3 *Class C12, 4–4–2T, No 67398 pauses at Grimoldby Station in June 1956*
                                                                Author's Collection

An entirely separate railway company, the Sutton and Willoughby, opened their line on 4 October 1886 from the East Lincolnshire Main Line at Willoughby, eight miles to Sutton on Sea, with one intermediate station, Mumby Road. They subsequently opened a three-mile extension to Mablethorpe on 14 September 1888.

In its early years traffic was light, indeed in 1906 a steam railcar was tried out but the machine was not a success; known locally as 'The Totty Train', it proved incapable of accomodating all the traffic on offer. Both lines were worked by the Great Northern Railway (GNR) who eventually took over both companies, the Sutton and Willoughby in 1902, and the Louth and East Coast in 1908.

Mention must be made of the scheme that might have been. In the early 1880s a proposal was mooted to build a dock at Sutton on Sea for both general cargo and fish. Indeed, the Sutton and Willoughby was promoted with this in mind. The idea was revived in 1891 with the proposal for the Lancashire, Derbyshire and East Coast Railway which would have linked the east and west coasts. Running powers were sought over the line from Willoughby to a junction at Mumby Road, from where a new line would run to the harbour south of the town, and the dock was to cost £700 000. The proposal finally died when the Great Central Railway bought the Lancashire, Derbyshire and East Coast Railway in January 1907, and opened their own dock at Immingham in 1912.

From the 1870s, most railway companies were quick to see the potential from the increasing affluence and leisure time of 'the man in the street', then just beginning routinely to take an annual week's holiday. The GNR were no exception, and they marketed their links with the Lincolnshire coastal towns in the

Figure 10.4 *Saltfleetby Station in 1962. Although this stretch of the line had closed in December 1960, the track was still* in situ, *and remarkably weed-free*
                                                                © Glenn Answer

industrial Midlands and in London. On summer weekends often normally sleepy branch lines would echo to the sound of a procession of packed trains taking their human cargo to be discharged onto a sandy beach for a day or a week. For example, on August Bank Holiday 1906, 5400 people took advantage of the three shillings (15p) return fare from Kings Cross to Mablethorpe, and the total for the summer was 92 000. Big business indeed.

Mablethorpe was always popular with people from the Nottingham area. From the early days there was a weekday through-train between the two, via Grantham and Boston. In

Figure 10.5 *GNR steam motor No 6 at Sutton on Sea in 1906. Known as 'The Totty Train' to the locals, it was not a success as there were too many passengers for its restricted accommodation*   Courtesy E Neve Collection

1890 it left Nottingham at 9.0 am, arriving at Mablethorpe at 11.34 am, and the return left at 6.10 pm (later retimed to 4.23), and this service operated until the outbreak of war in 1939. By 1914, on peak summer Saturdays, there were four return through-trains Nottingham–Mablethorpe, and one each from Leicester, Leeds and Bradford, and Manchester via Sheffield. In 1938 these services were very similar, although the Leicester train was replaced by one from Burton on Trent. There was also a Sunday train from Cleethorpes, leaving at 12.50 pm, to Sutton on Sea, returning at 8.27 pm.

The towns flourished and were encouraged to provide more and more of the seaside attractions the holidaymaker demanded. The traffic was so important that some lines, following closure to regular passenger traffic, still carried holiday excursion traffic during summer months. For example, the line to Leicester Belgrave Road lost its regular passenger service in 1957, but seasonal Saturday and Sunday excursion trains used it for another five years. In 1958 twenty-seven trains ran from here to Mablethorpe, and in 1959, twenty-eight.

The traffic was not confined to weekends, weekday specials also ran from Midland towns in their holiday weeks, but Sunday was the peak day. On the busiest days storage was a problem, and Mablethorpe's three carriage sidings were soon full. Goods sidings were then pressed into use, and finally the line north to Louth, on which no Sunday service ran was filled up with trains end to end. Many of the engines from these trains were too large for the small turntable, and they were despatched, three at a time, to Firsby, to be turned via the triangle there formed by the Skegness branch junctions. The greatest number of excursion trains in one day was August Bank Holiday Sunday, 1951, when there were nineteen. Retired railwaymen recall these days because of the organisation required for stabling to ensure the trains could leave in their booked order.

From the late 1950s, however, holiday fashions began to change, and increasingly the car and coach traffic became more important. The effect of this traffic, though, was to increase the importance of the southern half of the line from Willoughby,

which these trains used, and it became the principal junction station. Service trains connected with the main line here and it enjoyed a more frequent service than the northern half. For example, in 1938 there were only four trains each way throughout, with one each way from Sutton to Louth. The daily five each way from Sutton to Willoughby were increased to twelve each way on Saturdays.

The GNR built a small single-road engine shed at Mablethorpe and for many years a Stirling 0–4–2 tender locomotive was stationed there. Its day's work began at 8.0 am, taking empty coaches to Sutton on Sea for an 8.35 am train to Louth; after two trips back to Sutton and Louth, it then took a goods train to Willoughby, and it completed its day on a 4.45 pm passenger train to Mablethorpe. For a long time the engine was No 958, which was withdrawn from service in 1921 and replaced

Figure 10.7   The truncated remains of the line north of Mablethorpe Station in the spring of 1970. The service had been lost ten years before, and most of the track removed, but this short stub was left to be reclaimed by nature   © Author

Figure 10.6   Mablethorpe's once busy station, seen here in 1970, six months before closure. The train stands in Platform 2. Platform 3 is on the left, Platform 1 was a bay, in front of the signal box, for Louth trains. Several sidings off the north end of the station can be seen in the background. These were required for the heavy Midlands excursion traffic which arrived here from the 1870s to the 1950s   © Author

41

Figure 10.8 *The once proud and neat Mumby Road Station in 1971, nine months after closure. This tiny station was largely built of wood but even such a humble station as this had ornate barge boards with finials, an attractive platform canopy, and finely detailed brick chimney stacks* © Author

by Ivatt 4–4–2 tank, No 1506, but in 1924 the shed was closed. All branch workings were then undertaken from the shed at Louth.

The railway became a lifeline in 1953. On the night of 31 January a surge of water in the North Sea caught the east coast of England unawares and as night fell the dunes south of Sutton on Sea were breached. There was severe flooding, up to five feet deep in places, and several people were drowned. One Mablethorpe family escaped by using a plate-layer's trolley on the line. The whole area was evacuated and a battle began to close the gap through which successive tides continued to flood. The Army and civilian contractors were called in and between them they used 40 000 tons of Scunthorpe slag, brought by rail to Sutton on Sea over a two-week period, to stem the tide. Train loads were delivered to Alford, from where they were delivered, sixteen 12-ton wagon loads at a time.

The beginning of the end came on 5 December 1960 when the former Louth and East Coast Railway, and its intermediate stations, lost both passenger and goods services. The rails were removed the following year, but before this, on an occasion in the summer of 1961, a late night return-excursion to Lincoln had to traverse the route because of a derailment on the level-crossing at the south end of Mablethorpe Station. A short length was left, leading, overgrown and forlorn, northwards from Mablethorpe. Closure proposals for the rest of the branch came in 1963 with the Beeching Report, and although complete closure was fought off, the line lost its goods service on 30 June 1964. As a further economy measure pay-trains were introduced

in 1968, but even so, the line still enjoyed a good level of service, with eleven up- and ten down-trains a day.

The end finally came on 5 October 1970, when the branch closed completely. But it did not die unmourned: on the final day of full service, Saturday 3rd, passengers at Mablethorpe were greeted by a blackboard chalked with this elegy:

THIS DAY AND AGE – DEATHS
On October 3rd passed away at 7.55 pm after long illness the Mablethorpe–Willoughby British Railways Branch Line. Passed away but not peacefully.

> The time has come to close the line,
> for eighty years it served us fine,
> The loaded trains and car park too,
> Whilst we poor chaps had to work through.
> We've seen the passing of Station Masters,
> Old ones, new ones and now the few
> who will march en masse to get on the roll,
> and live happily ever after, on the dole.
> But cheer up folks, do not despair,
> Express Buses will get you there.
> Helicopters too, so we're told
> will fly you to Grimsby for a shopping load.
> Where's Beeching? You may well ask,
> Gone elsewhere, wielding his axe.

In the evening, a party of forty mourners in funereal clothing travelled from Mablethorpe to Sutton on Sea with a coffin. They alighted at Sutton and, with ceremony, burnt the coffin, before retiring to a local inn for suitable celebrations. So ended yet another of Lincolnshire's railways.

11

The Alford and Sutton Tramway

Tramways in the road were a common sight in Victorian towns, but there were very few rural examples. One of these, the only one in Lincolnshire, was the Alford and Sutton Tramway. It had a very short life, only five years and eight months, but it had too the unique distinction of a crossing, on the level, with a standard-gauge railway line.

From the 1870s the railway companies became adept at creating a market for day trips to places of interest, taking advantage of town workers' days off to provide cheap excursions which grew to become a very lucrative operation. The Great Northern Railway (GNR) opened their main line through Alford, and worked trains on the Louth and East Coast Railway from Louth to Mablethorpe from 1877. By this route excursion trains brought trippers to Mablethorpe, but at the time there was no standard gauge branch to Sutton on Sea.

The idea was born that there was a gap in the market. A link between Alford and Sutton on Sea would not only gain traffic from the two towns, and the villages in between, but would also help the development of Sutton on Sea by carrying excursionists there from the GNR's Alford Station.

Parliamentary approval was given in the 1880 session for a 2' 6" gauge tramway, and work began at the end of 1882. The line was single track, seven miles long, with passing loops, and the rails were laid in the road of what is now the A1111. Why a tramway and not a railway was chosen is not recorded, but cost is the likely answer, a separate standard-gauge line on its own reserved track being a more expensive proposition. The Act also empowered the Tramway to convey goods, in trucks attached to the coaches. Three vertical-boilered tram engines were purchased, and, after a few minor problems identified by the Board of Trade Inspectors had been righted, on 2 April 1884 it opened to the public.

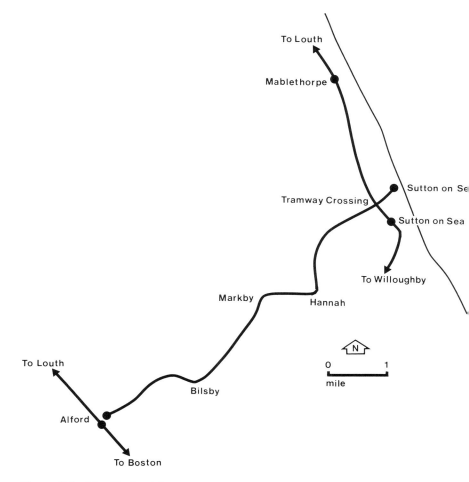

Figure 11.1 *The Alford and Sutton Tramway*

Figure 11.2 *The scene in Alford on the opening day, 2 April 1884*
Courtesy G Dow Collection

The opening was the cause of great celebration in Alford, where the streets were decorated with bunting, and all the shops closed for half the day. So many people wanted to travel that goods trucks were pressed into use as well.

At first the tramway was a success, indeed, a similar line was proposed from Alford to Skegness via Chapel St Leonards. However, while all this was going on, the Sutton and Willoughby Railway were preparing proposals for their stand-ard-gauge line to Sutton on Sea, and late in 1884 they cut the first sod. Two years later, in October 1886, the new line opened, and the writing was on the tramway wall!

In July 1888 the Mablethorpe–Sutton link was forged, giving rise to the unique *Tramway Crossing* where the narrow gauge road tramway crossed the standard-gauge railway line on a level-crossing. This was on the outskirts of Sutton on Sea, and the signal box here was always known by this name, intriguing coastal visitors by road and rail for eighty years after the tramway closed. It was to become the last obvious visible reminder of this unusual line.

Figure 11.3 *A mixed train, four trucks and one of the line's delightful coaches, hauled by Engine No 1, standing in the road outside Alford Town Station*
Courtesy G Dow Collection

The trams could not compete with the trains. After all, the two largest settlements they served both had their own railway station, and the intermediate villages were very small. For goods, traders preferred to deliver to and collect from the railway stations to avoid transhipment costs at either end. Inevitably the tramways days were numbered.

In December 1889 it closed. The people who had welcomed it with open arms five short years before no longer used it; the railway had killed it, just as in its turn, the railway would be killed by the internal combustion engine.

12

Louth to Bardney

Railways always fought shy of the Lincolnshire Wolds, a range of hills about eight miles wide rising to 550 feet at their highest point. To the south, east and west are low-lying flat areas only a little above sea level. Railways on these lower areas were soon constructed – the Wolds were surrounded by the end of 1848, but it took over twenty years for a line – the only line – to be built through this scenically attractive but sparsely populated area. Because of this it was to be in financial difficulty all its life.

Powers to construct the line were obtained in 1866 by the Louth and Lincoln Railway. Investors were attracted by forecasts of the large amounts of iron ore waiting in the area to be extracted; it was even forecast that blast furnaces would be built at Donington on Bain. None were, and no ore was ever to be quarried there either.

There were difficulties right from the start. Problems over land acquisition and local investment led to the Company asking the Board of Trade if the project could be abandoned. This was refused and the Company were committed. The situation was not helped by the steep gradients and heavy earthworks, including two tunnels, that were needed.

The first section of the line, from Bardney to South Willingham, was opened on 9 November 1874. This nine-mile stretch had intermediate stations at Kingthorpe and Wragby, the latter the only branch station with two platforms. The completion of the first tunnel, at South Willingham, enabled a three-mile extension to be opened to Donington on Bain on 27 September 1875. The final eight miles, including Withcall Tunnel, opened to goods on 26 June 1876, and 1 December the same year for passengers, with an intermediate station at Hallington. An initial service of five trains each way soon fell to four a month later.

In July 1882 a siding was opened at Withcall, followed by a station there on 1 August 1882. This was the year the line was acquired by the Great Northern Railway after falling into the hands of the Receiver.

In 1887 the service was four trains each way from Louth to Lincoln, calling at all stations, and taking one hour and twenty minutes for the journey. This was soon to be curtailed to four 50 minute Bardney–Louth services only each way. A forty-eight-foot turntable was installed at Bardney to turn the branch engines, but must have been little used for this purpose as contemporary photographs show engines pulling trains backwards as well as forwards.

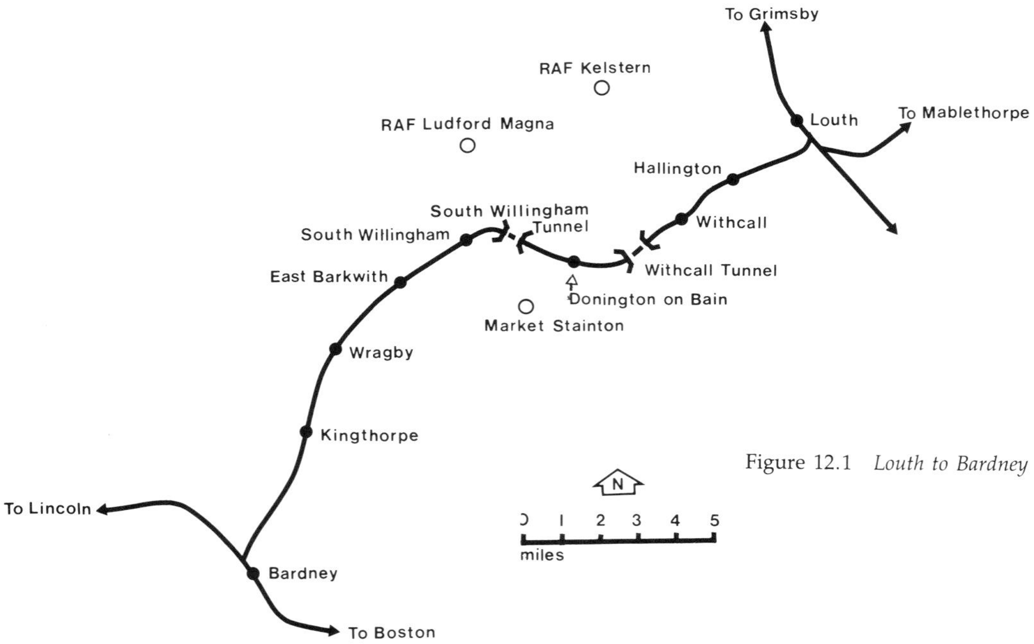

Figure 12.1 *Louth to Bardney*

46

Figure 12.2   *South Willingham signal box around the turn of the century, with a
goods train approaching from Louth*   Courtesy J Hickling

The only increase in activity on the line came in the Second World War. Lincolnshire became known as the Bomber County with the construction of many front-line airfields. Two of these were at Kelstern and Ludford Magna, and to serve them in January 1943 a Maintenance Unit, No 233, was formed in the area to store and supply bombs and other equipment. It was given the name of Market Stainton, but in fact comprised some sixty miles of roadside grass verges. The stations used to supply this were Donington on Bain, Withcall and Hallington. It was closed in 1948, and peace and tranquillity – and financial hardship – returned to the railway.

A dramatic episode occurred in October 1946 when a goods train to Louth of eleven wagons was approaching Donington on Bain Station. A spark from the engine ignited the straw packing of a truck laden with propane gas cylinders. The straw was burning fiercely but the guard and fireman successfully uncoupled the rear wagons. The train moved on, the burning wagon was detached, and the remainder of the train moved on again. Once isolated, the gas cylinders began exploding, causing the wagon to run back and set fire to coal wagons behind it. The guard and fireman were injured, and subsequently received bravery awards.

Disaster was narrowly averted on another occasion. The guard of a goods train carrying out shunting movements at South Willingham omitted to put on his van brake. As the van ran away towards Bardney, the guard had time to warn East Barkwith and Wragby Stations, and the gates there were hurriedly closed to road traffic. The van eventually came to rest a few yards short of Wragby.

Figure 12.4 Wragby Station in 1953 – the only branch station with two platforms. The distance between the level-crossing gates and the signal box can be appreciated. The delays this could cause to road traffic, because of the distance the signalman had to walk to close and open the gates, gave rise to many complaints Courtesy P Sutton

Figure 12.5   *Class C12 No 67379 pauses at Kingthorpe with a Louth train in 1950. Opened in 1874, this small, isolated station with its one siding, just visible to the rear of the second coach, could rarely have been busy. The passenger service between Louth and Bardney ceased from 3 November 1951, but goods trains continued to* run through Kingthorpe until 1960. The siding here was closed on 15 September 1956. *Engine 67379 was kept at Louth shed for over twenty years and was a frequent sight on the branch. Indeed, it was to haul the very last Louth–Bardney and return, service passenger train*

© E Steele

49

Figure 12.6 *Class C12 No 67379 at Bardney on 3 November 1951, with the last service passenger train to traverse the branch. From left to right are the Relief Stationmaster for Bardney, a Bardney Porter/Guard, the Fireman and Driver, the train Guard and another Bardney Porter/Guard. The Stationmaster at Wragby had placed the wreath on the engine when it paused there on its way to Bardney. The last journey to Louth was made immediately after this photograph was taken*

© G Nightscales

Wragby level-crossing was a constant source of complaints. The signal box was at the other end of the station from the level-crossing and on being notified of an approaching train, the signalman had to walk to work the gates and then come back to deal with the train. After it had passed, he had reset his signals, and then again take the long walk to open the road. All this took about eight minutes, during which time the exasperated motorists sat and fumed!

On 5 November 1951 the line lost its passenger service, the last trains running on Saturday 3 November. The very last train was hauled by C12, 4–4–2T, No 67379 of Louth shed, an engine that had been a regular sight on the branch trains (*see* Figure 12.5). On its smokebox it bore a wreath inscribed 'Louth Bardney Passenger Service, In Memoriam, Born 1876, Died 1951'. Extra coaches were added for the additional passengers who wished to travel, and in the growing darkness the passage of the last train was duly celebrated.

Goods traffic, however, continued ceasing only in stages, just as the line had opened: from 17 September 1956 Donington on Bain became the terminus of the line from Bardney; from 1 December 1958 Wragby became the railhead, with one train daily from Lincoln; and the final stretch closed on 1 February

Figure 12.7 *On 13 September 1956, a freight train pauses at Hallington Station for the Class A5 4–6–2T engine to shunt the single siding. On the following day the very last train passed through here before removal of the track. The line closed between Donington on Bain and Louth at the weekend, four days later*

Courtesy M White Collection

1960. By October of the following year the track was completely removed. Much of the line from Bardney to South Willingham has disappeared, incorporated into adjoining fields, but from there on its route may still be seen. Of the stations, only Kingthorpe has gone; the tiny waiting room at Withcall is now a Methodist chapel and the others serve as isolated country houses.

Figure 12.8   *The last goods train calls at Wragby, witnessed by a small group of people who came to pay their respects. From 1 December 1958 the station was the terminus of the branch from Bardney and closed on 1 February 1960. The engine was an A5 4–6–2 tank, built in August 1911 to a Robinson, Great Central design. Its home for its final years was at Lincoln, and it did not long survive the Wragby branch, going to the scrap-heap in November 1960*   © R Bones

13

The Lancashire, Derbyshire and East Coast Railway – Lincoln to Tuxford Section

The Lancashire, Derbyshire and East Coast Railway (LDECR), an independent concern until taken over by the Great Central Railway, was doomed never to reach Lancashire, or the east coast. It came quite late on the railway scene, and was, in fact, the last line to be built into Lincoln. Because of the geographical area considered in this book, the 14-mile eastern section of it, between Tuxford and Lincoln, is dealt with in detail.

It was in the early 1880s that a proposal was made to build a new east coast port at Sutton on Sea, to handle both fish and general cargo; a branch railway line to it from the East Lincolnshire Main Line at Willoughby was also proposed. The Sutton and Willoughby Railway was duly built, but no dock. However the idea was revived in 1891 in connection with a railway to run from Warrington in Lancashire to the proposed port, a distance of 171 miles, to give the Derbyshire coalfield additional outlets. It was always envisaged that the central section, through the coalfield, would be the most lucrative, and it was this on which construction commenced, from a terminus at Chesterfield Market Place, to Pyewipe Junction, two miles west of Lincoln Central Station.

This 58-mile length included, besides many cuttings and embankments, four great engineering features, the two viaducts at Chesterfield and at Doe Lea Valley near Bolsover, a third over the River Trent east of Fledborough (*see* Figure 13.3), which has four girder spans and fifty-nine brick arches, and fourthly the 2624-yard Bolsover Tunnel. The expenses were, in

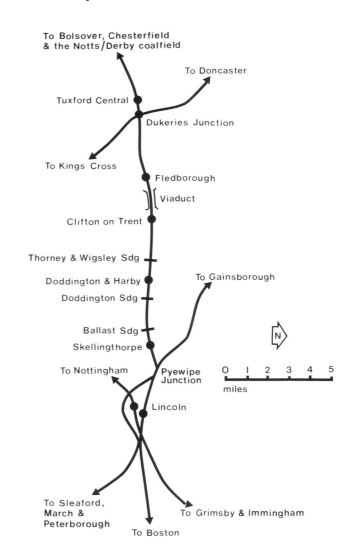

Figure 13.1 *The Lancashire, Derbyshire and East Coast Railway – Lincoln to Tuxford Section*

Figure 13.2 *On 25 July 1949, an A5 4–6–2 tank, No 69815 leaves Lincoln Central with the 12.45 pm to Chesterfield Market Place*   © D Swift

consequence, very high, and as capital was not being subscribed the extensions to the east and west were quietly dropped for the time being in 1894.

The double-track line opened for goods traffic on 16 November 1896, a passenger service between Lincoln and Edwinstowe started a month later from 15 December, and the line was opened throughout from 8 March in the following year. The eastern section had stations at Tuxford Town, later renamed Tuxford Central, Fledborough, Clifton on Trent, Doddington and Harby and Skellingthorpe. There were goods sidings at Thorney and Wigsley and at Doddington and a ballast pit siding halfway between Doddington Siding and Skellingthorpe, which was out of use by 1915.

The two public sidings were unstaffed; intended for coal and general merchandise in lots of one ton or over, for administrative and operational purposes they both came under the control of the Stationmaster at Doddington and Harby Station.

An indication of the standard of construction and economy of operation intended is gained from the fact that there were only two level-crossings on the route, at Bolsover and Skellingthorpe. These crossings were both sited where a signal box was to be built anyway, otherwise under- or overbridges were constructed, even for many farm crossings, all adding to the construction costs.

At Pyewipe Junction exchange sidings, which allowed transfer of wagons from one railway company to another, were constructed. Although the Great Eastern Railway (GER) had running powers over the line, and LDECR engines worked trains to Grimsby, these sidings were extremely busy – the lonely Pyewipe Inn, reached by a chain operated ferry across the Fossdyke Canal, became a favourite haunt for engine crews waiting for a return working. There was also a GER engine shed here, but one LDECR engine was kept here as well to work the sidings.

Figure 13.3 *Fledborough's impresssive viaduct – four girders span over the River Trent and fifty-nine brick arches carry the line over the flood plain* © Author

At Tuxford the main engine shed and workshop were sited. There were also brass and iron foundries, a boiler and wheel shop, an erecting and paint shop and a carpentry department for coaches and wagons; Tuxford had the largest engine shed on the system, houses were built for the employees, and a railway community was created.

Whilst coal was the main reason for construction of the line, right from the start the company had high hopes of a busy tourist traffic. The line passed through the Dukeries, that part of Sherwood Forest within which lie the great estates of Clumber Park, Thoresby Hall and Welbeck Abbey, and taking their cue from this the company promoted the line as 'the Dukeries Route'.

The most interesting manifestation of this were the Dukeries Junction High- and Low-Level Stations, originally named Tuxford Exchange, opened on 1 June 1897. At the point one mile east of Tuxford, where the line crossed the Great Northern, on an overbridge, an interchange station was constructed. The High-Level Station was an island platform actually on the bridge itself, connected to the Great Northern Low-Level Station by a stairway. The Low-Level Station was itself only half a mile south of Tuxford Great Northern Station. The Company constructed a Stationmaster's house by the High-Level Station, approached by footpath across the fields from Tuxford village. Both Tuxford stations were better placed to serve the village, and the Junction was designed to facilitate interchange of passengers between trains only. It saw little use, however. By 1938 three trains each way between Lincoln and Chesterfield stopped there, but only one each way on the main line. In addition, one each way would stop if the guard had been notified previously. These

Figure 13.4 *Doddington and Harby Station in 1968. The building on the right was the Stationmaster's house. This arrangement was typical of the smaller stations on the line, the platform having only a single-storey building with the waiting room and so on* © Richard Goodman

The Great Central assumed control from 1 January 1907. They continued promotion of 'the Dukeries Route', instituted a Grimsby to Leicester through-train and made holiday and excursion traffic a regular feature.

At the beginning there were four freight trains each way daily. This had risen to seventy-five each way daily by 1907. Coal was carried from Derbyshire and Nottinghamshire to Immingham and Grimsby for export, and to London and the south via March Whitemoor or Peterborough, New England. In 1964 there were, weekly, fifty-seven freight trains each way to Whitemoor, thirty-five each way to Grimsby or Immingham, and forty-four each way to New England. By 1980 this had fallen to four eastbound and five westbound, daily.

The first closures were Dukeries Junction High- and Low-Level Stations on 6 March 1950. From 3 December 1951 the east

Figure 13.5 *Diesel locomotive 31.281 arriving at Skellingthorpe with a train of empty coal trucks as it returns to Mansfield from Frodingham, on 22 July 1976. The speed-limit sign to the left of the train marks the end of the double-track section from Pyewipe Junction. This signal box remained after the track was removed, and there were hopes that it would be saved as an example of the village's railway heritage. It suffered heavy vandalism, however, and was finally demolished in August 1985*

© P Grey

Figure 13.6 *Dukeries Junction, High and Low Level Stations c 1910*

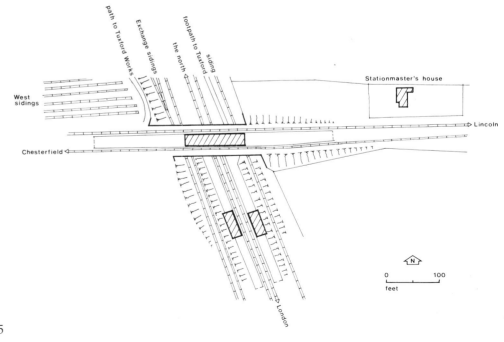

trains were local only – no long-distance trains called, and for both the main use was by railway staff going to and from Tuxford Works.

The initial service was of four trains each way daily between Lincoln and Chesterfield but in later years this fell to three. There was never a Sunday service, as this had been ruled out from the start by the Dukeries landowners.

Figure 13.7   *The demolition train near Doddington, hauled by a Class 08 diesel shunter, on 11 August 1981. The Doddington Goods Siding was on the far side of the railway bridge behind the rear of the train*
© P Grey

end was closed because of the poor state of Bolsover Tunnel, and passenger trains terminated at Shirebrook. On 19 September 1955, regular passenger traffic ceased and the stations were closed to travellers. Tuxford Central also lost its goods service. On 30 March 1964 the stations and goods sidings other than Fledborough lost their freight service, the latter following on 4 January 1965.

The coal traffic continued, as did seasonal passenger excursions to Skegness and Mablethorpe; the 1964 summer timetable shows four trains, from Radford, Nottingham, Sheffield and Manchester, to the Lincolnshire and Yorkshire coasts, on Saturdays, and three in the opposite direction. But these services ceased from 6 September 1964; occasional colliery outings to the coast, routed via Lincoln, continued into the late 1970s. The very last passenger train was a South Yorkshire Railtour, which passed this way eastbound in the evening, on 17 May 1979.

There was a renaissance of traffic when High Marnham Power Station opened in 1962, south of Fledborough Station, and the line to here is still being used today by merry-go-round trains of coal. The eastern end of the line, from Fledborough to Skellingthorpe, was singled in 1963, and the semaphore signals were replaced by coloured lights.

The end came rather suddenly on 5 July 1980, when a Thoresby Colliery, Nottinghamshire, to March Whitemoor coal train was derailed, because of a wagon defect, approaching Clifton on Trent Station. The track was badly damaged and the decision was taken to close the line rather than carry out repairs. The track from Fledborough Station to Pyewipe Junction was removed the following year.

14

Lincoln St Marks

The line from Nottingham to Lincoln St Marks, opened on 3 August 1846, was the first railway line in Lincolnshire; it was also the last to be closed as far as this book is concerned.

The first proposal for a line between the two cities was mooted in 1834; authority was given in 1845, and the thirty-three miles of line took only ten months to build. Lincoln St Marks was the terminus, taking its name from a nearby church, and being built on the site of an ancient graveyard associated with the White-friars. It is an impressive building, of Grecian style, which it is hoped to preserve in the forthcoming redevelopment of the area.

The first steam train arrived, unannounced, in June 1846 but the townspeople flocked to see it as word got around. The official opening, two months later, was the first of many occasions for county celebrations connected with the construction of railways. This one was special, however – the first opening and in the county town. The day was declared a holiday; the shops closed and people from town and country flocked to gaze in awe at the wonder of the age.

St Marks did not remain a terminus for long. An end-on connection at the High Street was made with the Manchester, Sheffield and Lincolnshire Railway, later the Great Central, when they opened the last remaining section of their line to Grimsby via Barnetby Junction on 18 December 1848. It was this company who built the unique single-storey, brick, octagonal signal box, across the High Street from the station, which worked the level-crossing gates. They also provided a goods shed, sidings and a coal yard, on land immediately east of the level-crossing. An unusual situation arose from this connection, as the Up-line of the Midland Railway became the Down-line of the Great Central at the level-crossing. Great care had to be

Figure 14.1   *Lincoln St Marks*

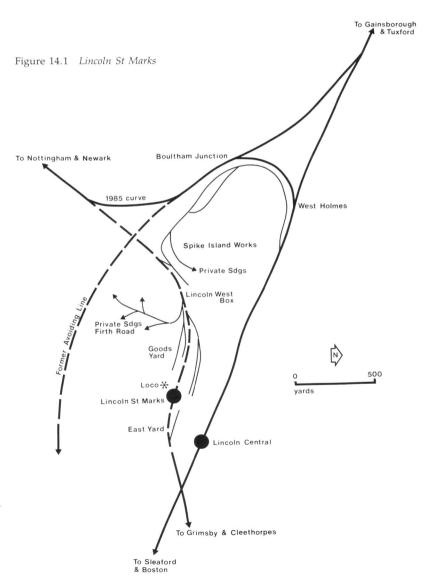

taken with the issuing of instructions over 'wrong-line' working when engineering work caused the temporary closure of one line of rails through the station.

The Midland Railway provided a goods yard to the north of the station, a two-road engine shed adjacent to it on the south side, and further sidings to the south of the running lines on the station approaches.

As a city at the heart of a great agricultural county, Lincoln attracted a number of engineering firms, at first producing farming equipment, but which soon grew to manufacture a great variety of machinery of all forms. Foremost amongst these was that established by Joseph Ruston in 1854. It was, over the years, known by a number of names, but is probably most usually referred to as 'Ruston and Hornsby'. There were a number of parts to the factory complex, on both sides of the

Figure 14.2 *Lincoln West signal box and the Ropewalk level-crossing in 1955. In the background is evidence of how busy a railway goods yard could be at that time, all the sidings full with a variety of open wagons and closed vans. Behind these is the two-road engine shed and the overall roof of St Marks Station. The tall building to their left was the Midland goods shed. The photograph also illustrates the private lines and sidings associated with the railway here. In the foreground are the buffer stops of two of the sidings serving Ruston and Hornsby's Spike Island Works to the west of the line, and, in the centre, beyond the signal box, what was probably one of the diesel locomotives built by Ruston and Hornsby. It is standing on the line that served the company's works, and others, off Firth Road. One of the sidings can be seen curving away from the rear of the locomotive, and, after running through the large building on the right, reappearing to make an unguarded crossing of the road*   Courtesy *Lincolnshire Echo*

Figure 14.3 *A train of eight Cavalier tank conversions awaits removal from the private sidings outside the Ruston and Hornsby Works in 1945. The conversion was a Ruston design, for use as an artillery observation vehicle, weighing twenty-six tons, of which 220 were built by this firm. They stand alongside Firth Road outside Cannon's Glue Works. The tanks were loaded from the ramp at the rear of the train and driven along the trucks before being chained and sheeted down*   © R Hooley

removed soon after, the rails alongside Firth Road could be seen until they were removed in 1987.

St Marks became Lincoln's main station in 1965 when the line from Lincoln Central to Grantham via Honington closed. Prior to this the connections with London ran from Central; now they ran from St Marks and connected at Newark Northgate. Direct through-trains from Grimsby and Cleethorpes also passed this way.

Closure of St Marks, together with almost a mile of track, came about not because the level of traffic could not justify its continued existence, but because of a much needed rationalisation of railway facilities in the Lincoln area. Central Station

Figure 14.4 *'Stanier Black 5', 4–6–0 No 44919, arrives at Lincoln St Marks with a Saturday excursion from the Midlands to Cleethorpes in 1960. The station had, until 1957, an overall roof. The temporary canopy which replaced it, supported by scaffolding seen to the right of the engine, was subsequently replaced by a more conventional awning. The vehicle standing on the left is a Travelling Post Office, with a side corridor*   © Richard Goodman

Figure 14.5 *Another 'Black 5', No 44661, threads its way through Lincoln East Yard with an excursion from the Midlands to Cleethorpes on 26 June 1961*
© Richard Goodman

railway, and all were rail-connected; the factories used their own engines on them. The premises of the firm William Foster, who built the first tank, were established off Firth Road also in the 1850s and Cannon's Glue Factory in 1874, and further sidings were built to these. The Midland Railway became the focus for a large network of industrial railway lines, along which flowed much of these factories' exports. The last traffic to use the southern connection was a trainload of diesel engines from the Ruston Works in 1968. Although the connection was carrying a commemorative headboard. The station was crowded with travellers paying their last respects, and 139 years of service came to an end. The rails were removed in June and July 1985, but the station still stands, hopefully to be incorporated into any future redevelopment scheme for the site.

Figure 14.6   *St Marks on 5 May 1985, the last Sunday of operation. A train from Grimsby stands at Platform 2, while at Platform 1 a Nottingham train has just arrived. The station was once more imposing, with an overall roof covering not only the platforms, but both the two central sidings as well. The latter terminated at the High Street, the running lines only crossing the road*   © Author

Figure 14.7   *Track-removal in the pouring rain on 7 June 1985. The former Ruston and Hornsby's Spike Island Works are to the left of the train, and there was once a connection to them, although latterly the works were reached by a siding parallel to British Rail from West Holmes to Boultham Junction*   © Author

was much larger and could cope better with the traffic of the 1980s and beyond, and the rearrangement would remove one of the city's major traffic problems, one of the two level-crossings over the High Street. A £1.7 million scheme to construct a short length of new line enabling the diversion of all traffic into a renovated Central Station was opened on 12 May 1985 and St Marks closed.

The last trains ran on 11 May, the last train from Nottingham

15

The Lincoln Avoiding Line

The new Lincoln Bypass opened in December 1985 and was welcomed by the residents of the city because of the reduction of traffic in the city centre. But this was not the first Lincoln Bypass; there was an earlier one, of the railway age, and, had it not been built, city centre congestion could have been even worse.

Lincoln is sited strategically at the point where the River Witham cuts through the Lincoln Edge, and since Roman times has been an important town, the focal point of routes north and south over the heathland and east and west through the Trent and Witham Valleys.

Just as in earlier days roads had been built radiating from the city, in the nineteenth century the railways came to use the same gap, crossing existing roads on the level. By 1870 water, road and rail routes were competing within limited space and creating congestion, congestion that was apparent even from the early railway days, and was for over a hundred years the subject of great debate by the citizens.

By 1870 railways radiated from the city's two stations to Nottingham, Grantham, Boston, Grimsby, Gainsborough and Retford and fierce competition was building up to provide a new route linking the South Yorkshire Coalfield with London. This led to the birth of the Great Northern and Great Eastern Joint Railway. (*See* Chapter 31.) Created partly by taking over existing routes and partly by linking these existing routes with new lengths, this line was to pass through the city, and great prospects were envisaged for it. Indeed, it did become an important route, enabling traffic to be carried to and from London and the North, leaving the East Coast Main Line clear for prestigious express services.

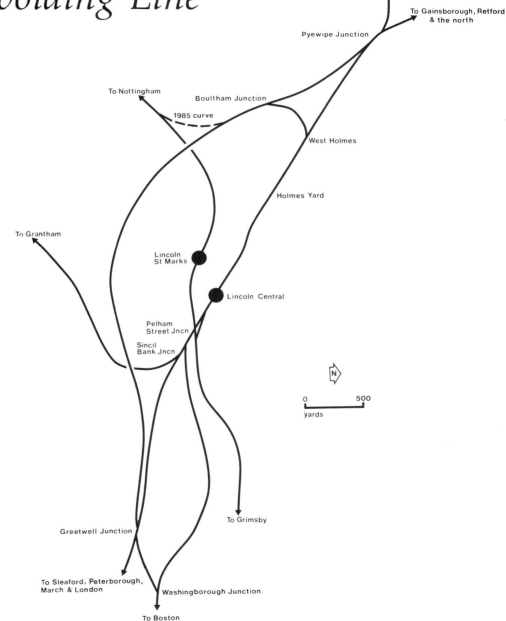

Figure 15.1 *The Lincoln Avoiding Line*

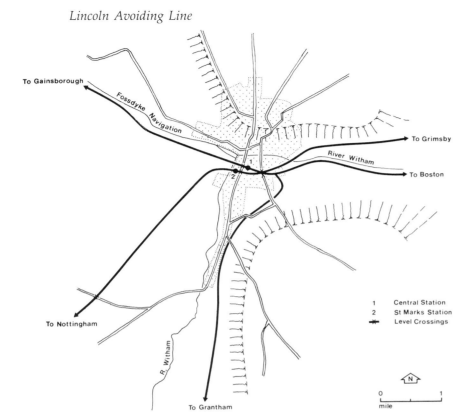

a curve between West Holmes and Boultham Junction, to enable trains from the south to use the line to reach the Holmes Goods Yard, and a short link eastwards from Greetwell Junction with the Sleaford Line, to Washingborough Junction on the Boston Line, which enabled trains from the west, bound for Boston and the coast, to use the route; coastal excursion traffic as well as some goods trains used this link.

The line was three miles long, double track throughout and subject to a 30 mph speed limit. Carried for most of its length on an embankment, a particular feature of the line was the number of girder bridges over the existing roads, railways and waterways of the city, most of them in very prominent locations which guaranteed their use as advertisement billboards.

The line was always well used, although as goods and passenger traffic fell over the years, the number of trains using it fell also. The last main users were the coal trains from the former Lancashire, Derbyshire and East Coast Railway from

Figure 15.3 Boultham Junction on 30 April 1965. Lincoln steam locomotive depot had closed in 1964, and the turntable was taken out of use. Steam engines continued to work into the city from the west for some time afterwards, using the Pyewipe Junction/West Holmes/Boultham Junction triangle to turn. Here B1 4–6–0 No 61360 is turning, after working a goods train from Doncaster. Having reversed from West Holmes along the line on the left, it is proceeding towards Pyewipe. The tracks on the left, below the embankment, are the private sidings serving the Ruston's Spike Island Works   © *Richard Goodman*

Figure 15.2 Lincoln – showing roads and railways radiating from the city in 1870

Such an increase in the number of trains through the city would create additional unacceptable problems, and as part of the proposal to build a line from Lincoln to Sleaford, the Lincoln-Avoiding Line was mooted.

It was opened in 1882 as part of the Great Northern and Great Eastern Joint Line, principally for Joint Line trains which did not need to stop in the city. For crew- and engine-changing purposes, the Great Eastern Railway established their motive-power depot at Pyewipe Junction. Additional refinements were

all the signal box's main equipment had been stolen. Six months later the track was removed.

The western end to the line still survives in use, although at a lower level than before. A new curve from the Nottingham Line was built north-westwards to the route of the Avoiding Line to enable St Marks Station to be closed and all traffic concentrated on Lincoln Central. (*See* Chapter 14 for further details of this.)

Figure 15.4   *A north-bound High Speed Train, diverted because of engineering work on the main line, crosses the longest railway bridge in Lincoln – that over the River Witham – on 6 February 1982*   © P Grey

Figure 15.5   *K1 2–6–0, No 62018 crossing the Lincoln–Grantham line on 2 March 1957 with a train of coal empties from March. At the time, this engine was allocated to March shed, along with 24 others of the class. It was withdrawn from Frodingham depot in March 1964*   © R E Burdon

Pyewipe Junction westwards through Tuxford, to March White-moor marshalling yard or Peterborough, New England. This traffic ceased in 1980. (*See* Chapter 13.)

The rationalisation of Lincoln's railways, culminating in the closure of St Marks Station in 1985 made the Avoiding Line redundant and it was closed in October 1983. Its passing was marked by an example of modern vandalism: within two hours of the final closing down of Greetwell Junction Box at 5.00 pm,

16

Lincoln to Honington Junction

This was Lincolnshire's royal railway line. For twenty years from the Second World War the Royal Train was a frequent overnight visitor to Leadenham Station. Journeys to and from the north where an overnight stop was required would see the train stabled on the long siding by the goods shed, alongside the main road. It was said that this site was first chosen for safety reasons, as a line of trees overhung this siding shielding the train from aerial view.

Built by Sleaford contractors Kirk and Parry, and comprising eighteen miles of double track, the line was opened on 15 April 1867. Stations were built at Waddington, Harmston, Navenby, Leadenham and Caythorpe, and at Honington on the Grantham to Sleaford line, previously opened on 16 June 1857. At Leadenham and Fulbeck all buildings and bridges were built of Ancaster stone, a condition imposed by the local landowners; cheaper red brick was used elsewhere and for the goods shed

Figure 16.1 *Lincoln to Honington Junction*

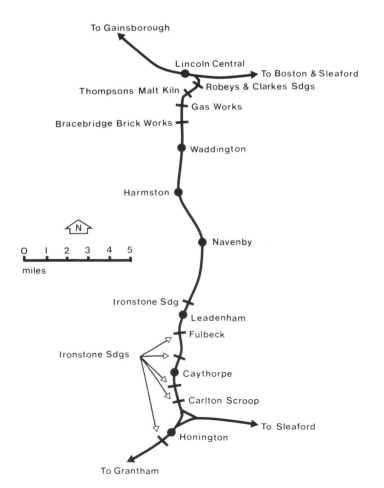

Figure 16.2 *The line was often used as a diversion route for main line trains on Sundays to allow engineering work to take place. Here a southbound express with Class A1, 4–6–2, No 60140,* Balmoral, *at its head passes through Waddington Station on 16 April 1961*
© R E Burdon

at Leadenham, which lay in Welbourn Parish within which the Leadenham landowner had no say.

George Hussey Packe, who was at the time the Chairman of the Great Northern Railway Company (GNR), lived at Caythorpe Hall. Because of this at Caythorpe Station he had his own personal waiting room and specially raised platforms and he had the right to have stopped any train passing through Caythorpe Station.

The day before the public opening, a special train carried the Mayors of Lincoln, Grantham, Boston and Newark, together with many other invited guests over the new line. For the occasion, Caythorpe goods shed was provided with a deal floor and festooned with evergreens and bunting, and a cold buffet was provided.

The new route cut three quarters of an hour off the journey time between Lincoln and London. There were five trains each way between Lincoln and Grantham, with two on Sundays. By 1887 this had risen to nine each way, but only one each way on Sundays. In 1914 there were six weekday trains from Lincoln to Grantham, of which two, the 11.22 am and the 1.50 pm conveyed through-carriages to London, Kings Cross. From London through-carriages ran on the 12.30 and 4.0 pm trains. In 1938 seven trains each way were normally run but only one through-carriage service to London. This ran on the 10.28 am from Lincoln to Grantham, where it was attached to the express from Newcastle due into Kings Cross at 1.15 pm. Return was by the 5.50 pm London to Yorkshire express, reaching Grantham at 7.55 pm. It left Grantham at 8.3 pm, called at Leadenham on request to set down passengers from London only, and was due into Lincoln at 8.37 pm. Not all trains stopped at all stations; usually one or two each way were Lincoln–Grantham direct to connect with main-line services. Most timetables show that if no scheduled stop was made at Leadenham, then some would stop to pick up or set down there if required.

From the opening of the line until the direct Lincoln to Slea-ford line opened in 1882, there was a north-to-east junction at Honington to allow through-running between the two towns.

Figure 16.3   *Caythorpe Station in April 1967, before its track was lifted and the station and signal box demolished. Caythorpe was once a proud and very busy scene. It was the local station for the Chairman of the Great Northern Railway, who regularly used it – that must have kept the staff on their toes! It was also the hub of the iron-ore quarrying in the area, and around the turn of the century up to three trainloads a day were despatched from sidings which ran behind the signal box. In its later years Caythorpe Station was the destination of the daily pick-up goods from Lincoln serving stations on the branch, which terminated here, unless, on rare occasions, there were wagons for collection or delivery to Honington*   © Author

This was removed after a life of some fifteen years.

The construction of the line in Caythorpe Parish revealed the existence of workable quantities of iron-ore almost on the surface. The exploitation of this ore over the next eighty years

Figure 16.4 *Leadenham Station in 1938, with the staff busy preparing for the Best Kept Station competition. Most railway companies promoted such competitions to encourage the staff to make their charge as attractive as possible for the travelling* *public. Over the years many Lincolnshire stations won awards and their certificates were always proudly displayed in ticket offices and waiting rooms*

Courtesy *Lincolnshire Echo*

is considered in greater detail in the next chapter. Suffice it to say here that rail-served quarries were worked at Leadenham, Fulbeck, Caythorpe, Carlton Scroop and Honington.

Each station had its goods sidings, busy mainly with local agricultural traffic and coal. In addition to these, sidings were provided at the northern end of the line for a number of purposes. Prior to the line's being built private sidings had been built to Robey's works and to Clarkes Crank and Forge, in Lincoln; now these were reconnected to the Honington line. New industries were attracted because the line gave them the opportunity to become rail-connected. At Bracebridge and at Waddington Station sidings were laid to brickworks, and in Lincoln, to Thompson's Malt Kiln. In 1874 the Lincoln Gas Works opened adjacent to the line with extensive coal-reception sidings on both sides of the track. It is likely that the Bracebridge brickworks was opened by the contractors to provide bricks for the line's buildings. Certainly it was owned by Kirk and Parry shortly after the line opened.

In 1897 the line was used for an experiment with an early form of semi-automatic train control invented by Mr Wynford Brierly. A two-lever trip connected to a bell was placed beside the cab footstep on Stirling 2–2–2 No 6 and this contacted a rocker actuated by signal wire near the signals. When at danger the signal rocker engaged the lever on the locomotive, ringing a bell in the cab and displaying a red disc below it. Although the trial proved to be successful the system was never installed on the GNR.

Accidents were rare, but there are records of three on this line. The worst of these – indeed one of the worst ever in the whole area was at Bracebridge Gas Works on 25 January 1963. At 11.00 am a B1 4–6–0 steam locomotive carrying out shunting movements was standing on the down main line. A diesel multiple unit travelling towards Lincoln struck it in the rear, killing two crew members in the cab. The driver of the steam engine, realising a collision was imminent, released his brakes, and this lessened the effect, probably saving the lives of passengers in the train.

Figure 16.5 *An 04 Class 2–8–0, No 63615 arriving at Bracebridge Gas Sidings with a coal train for the works on 10 February 1961. There were sidings on both sides of the line, those on the up side can be seen. The works themselves were off to the left of the photograph, and coal from the up sidings was carried to the works by the overhead conveyor* © Richard Goodman

Leadenham was the scene of another mishap, when a train struck a herd of beasts which had strayed onto the track. Sixteen were killed or had to be destroyed, but no injuries to people are recorded, and the train stayed on the rails.

The third event occurred at Caythorpe in 1943, when an RAF Lancaster crashed into the goods yard.

In the mid–1950s steam-hauled passenger trains were replaced with diesel multiple units on this line, one of the first routes on which this happened. Steam services were restored on some trains for a time in 1963 when Lincoln multiple units

Figure 16.6   Lincolnshire railway lines were among the first to be modernised in the mid-1950s with the introduction of diesel railcars. One of the first two-car sets is seen here in its early days travelling towards Grantham at Fulbeck   © *Author*

were taken temporarily to dieselise the Grantham to Nottingham service. The local goods trains remained steam-hauled to the end.

Leadenham was always the busiest and most important station, retaining its services when, on 10 September 1962, Honington, Caythorpe, Navenby and Waddington Stations closed for passenger and parcels traffic. On the same day Harmston closed completely. Two years later, on 15 June 1964, all stations lost their goods services other than for coal. This meant that only Leadenham retained a passenger service; in 1964 8700 tickets were issued or collected. Coal deliveries only were made to both Waddington and Leadenham – coal traffic was important in local terms: in 1964 Leadenham received

147 wagonloads. Occasional other consignments were delivered here also, and in 1965, just prior to closure, the yard looked busier than it had done for many years when truckloads of steel were delivered for the construction of electricity pylons in the area.

It was at this time, surprisingly, that the line enjoyed its best passenger service: the summer 1964 timetable included ten

Figure 16.7   Grantham locomotive shed closed in September 1963 and its engines were dispersed, either for service elsewhere, or for scrapping. Two 02 2–8–0s from Grantham, numbers 63940, and 63945, which were formerly mainly used on the Highdyke ironstone branch, are shown here, passing through Navenby on 11 September on the way to their new home at Doncaster   © *Richard Goodman*

trains each way, with three on Sundays, whereas for many years in the 1930s and 1940s there were no Sunday trains at all.

Closure to all traffic came on 1 November 1965. For a short time after one mile of track was retained northwards from Honington Junction and used for redundant wagon storage, and until 7 December 1970 the short section from Lincoln to the Gas Works was retained; the last rails were removed one year later.

Figure 16.8   Leadenham's very last ticket, carried by the last passenger to use the station on the last train from Lincoln
© Author

Figure 16.9   The truncated remains of the line at its southern end viewed from the A607 road bridge at Carlton Scroop on 16 April 1967. The final mile of track from Honington Junction was at this time being used for the storage of unused mineral wagons. Off to the left are the earthworks of the erstwhile north-to-east curve which was in use from 1867 to 1882, allowing direct running between Lincoln and Sleaford
© Richard Goodman

17

Ironstone Railways of the Lincoln Cliff

The construction of the railway line between Lincoln and Honington Junction in the 1860s revealed the existence of workable quantities of iron-ore in the Caythorpe area. For almost eighty years, 1870 to 1946, numerous quarries were exploited and all, without exception, were served by the railway line, by means either of short lengths of siding, or of more substantial lengths of track up to a mile in length. In addition, one used a cable-incline to reach the standard gauge and another – at Honington – had its own 3' gauge tramway (although rail access at Honington was actually gained not from this but from the Grantham–Sleaford Line, which remains open). Only one quarry had its own locomotive, the others were all worked by the Great Northern Railway and its successor, the London and North Eastern Railway.

17.1 The Ironstone Quarries

(a) *Caythorpe and Fulbeck*

The land on which the first deposits were discovered was owned by George Hussey Packe of Caythorpe Hall. At the time he was the Chairman of the Great Northern Railway Company, and he began quarrying on his land north of Caythorpe Station, to the west of the railway line. These workings moved progressively westwards to the main road, now the A607, and northwards towards Fulbeck. Initially a siding giving access was provided immediately north of the station. This area was later leased to the Stanton Ironworks Company.

In 1876 the West Yorkshire Iron and Coal Company leased land to the east of the railway line, north of Caythorpe Station. Their area extended northwards to a point south of the Fulbeck level-crossing. South of this crossing, the line passed over a small stream on a high embankment, and a siding, controlled by Fulbeck South signal box, was built from a point at the south

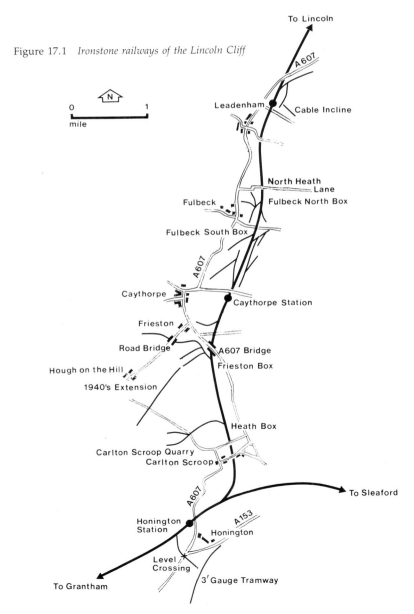

Figure 17.1 *Ironstone railways of the Lincoln Cliff*

end of the embankment to serve the quarry. The quarry lines extended parallel to the railway line almost to Caythorpe Station. In addition, another siding, controlled by the same signal box, was put in at this junction, to the west of the line for the quarry on that side as it extended northwards. By 1912 the workings to the east of the line were worked out, those to the west in about 1920.

At Caythorpe Station sidings were laid by the up platform for the stone traffic. In 1897 two trains a day were despatched, one to Ardsley leaving at 11.0 am and one to Colwick at 4.40 pm. Two additional trains ran when necessary at 12.40 pm to Doncaster, and at 6.28 pm to Colwick. These workings were balanced by two trains of empties, arriving from New England at 7.50 am and 9.20 am from Colwick. Two additional trains ran as required, arriving from New England at 8.40 am, and Colwick at 1.30 pm. By 1902 three regular daily trains were despatched.

Around 1908, as these deposits were being worked out, quarrying was extended into land north of Fulbeck level-crossing, east of the railway line, and a siding was put in for it protected by Fulbeck North signal box. Ore was also extracted to the west of the line, almost up to the North Heath Lane at Fulbeck. This was permitted by Colonel Fane, the landowner – despite it entering the parkland associated with his home – as a philanthropic gesture to retain local employment after the First World War – for many years he had consistently resisted pressure to exploit the stone here. He extracted a toll of one farthing per ton of excavated ore carried from the land. The stone was worked by hand and twelve to fifteen wagons were filled by the quarrymen daily. Working ceased in 1930.

Only slight traces of this remain today: the stone bed was about eight feet thick and near the surface; a careful look over the fields to the east of the A607 will reveal that their surface is six feet or so below that of road level, and to the east of the railway line is a narrow gullet at the foot of the escarpment, known locally as the Yorkshire Pit, where these workings ceased because of the hillside. Trial holes were again sunk here in 1953 to determine whether it would be worth reopening the quarry but this never happened.

(b) *Caythorpe and Frieston*

In April 1880 a signal box and sidings were built half a mile south of Caythorpe Station, north of the Frieston level-crossing, for a quarry between the railway line and the A607, and here ore was loaded by hand directly into railway trucks. Worked by the Stanton Ironworks Company from 1883, the quarry was exhausted in 1897. There is, however, evidence that quarrying also took place on the eastern side of the line adjacent to the southern edge of the station limits.

Around the time of the First World War another quarry was opened to the south of Frieston village by W Burke & Co. Sidings were laid from a point just south of the A607 road bridge, and an extensive quarry system radiated from this point. The workings gradually spread northwards, eventually bridging beneath the Frieston to Hough road.

In 1936 an 0–4–0 saddle tank, named *Munition* and built in 1918 by Hawthorn Leslie, was purchased for use in this quarry. This was to be the only privately owned engine to work in the quarries in the area; the rest were all worked by the GNR. It was painted green, lined in black edged with white, and lettered 'W Burke, Caythorpe Ironstone Mines'. It was housed in a small shed adjacent to the flooded former workings, the latter can be seen today. Upon closure of the system this engine was sold to Blackwell Colliery in Derbyshire. From 1930 to 1933, prior to *Munition* being purchased, a Class Y3 0–4–0 Sentinel geared shunting engine was used by the London and North Eastern Railway here, and this engine, No 49, worked the daily branch freight from Grantham, its home depot, to Waddington, and return, with two hours spent shunting the quarry sidings.

Also in 1936, Mr Burke introduced mechanical excavators into the quarries here, ending the fifty-year old practice of all stone being worked and loaded by hand.

During the Second World War, to meet an increasing demand for iron-ore, the quarry railway was extended for about a mile,

Figure 17.2　*The flooded Caythorpe and Frieston workings today, adjacent to the A607 south of Frieston village. Only the fence in the foreground marks the route of the Lincoln to Honington line, the road bridge being hidden in the bushes on the right-hand side of the photograph. This is the site of the junction with the quarry sidings, the latter ran away from this point, one siding passing between the two lakes*
© *Author*

across the fields, to an extension of the long abandoned Carlton Scroop workings. Laid without earthworks it had some severe gradients, up which *Munition* could only haul two loaded or four empty wagons. The line served no imtermediate quarry.

The Frieston system did not survive for long after the War. The rich beds of ore had long been exhausted, and in 1946 the workers were made redundant and the system closed. It was to be the last of the quarries in the area.

Considerable evidence remains to this day to locate them. The earliest workings are the two permanently flooded areas to the west of the A607 road bridge over the route of the Honington line south of the village. The Frieston–Hough road bridge still survives, rebuilt in recent years by the County Council, and on either side of it are sunken fields, with steep banks indicating the final limits of the quarries.

As an interesting postscript, *Munition* had a sister, supplied to the Ministry of Defence, which had a chequered career. Sent to the Singapore dockyard, it was captured and used by the Japanese until liberated in 1945. It was brought back to England, and after retirement found its way to the Rutland Railway Museum at Cottesmore. It is now named *Singapore*, and steamed occasionally to help keep alive the history of ironstone quarrying in the area.

(c) *Carlton Scroop*

Written evidence of the quarries here is difficult to find. What is known is that in the early 1900s a quarry was being worked by the West Yorkshire Iron and Coal Company, to the west of

Figure 17.3　*The remnants of the route of the railway line and siding at Carlton Scroop. The main running lines ran through the cutting, with the siding on the top of the embankment adjacent to it. Heath Box was at the far end where the cutting ended. The quarry line ran along the front of the hedge in the middle distance on the left-hand side of the photograph*
© *Author*

the road from Carlton Scroop to Hough. A siding with a signal box, Heath Box, was laid on the west side of the railway line, north of the northernmost railway bridge at Carlton Scroop. From this a branch, one mile long, ran westwards, around the north side of the Hall, to the quarry. It had been closed by the time of the First World War, and the track had been removed by the early 1920s. Evidence of the siding can be seen alongside the cutting through which the Honington line ran, where once stood the signal box, and a shallow cutting can be noted on either side of the Carlton Scroop to Hough road, a few yards west of Carlton Scroop Hall.

As mentioned previously, some further quarrying took place here during World War Two, ore being removed via the Frieston railway system, but this proved to be a brief renaissance, only brought about by the unique demand for iron and steel caused by these, fortunately unusual, circumstances.

(d) *Honington*

Honington Quarry was opened by the Stanton Ironworks Company in 1901. It was below the western edge of the hillside east of the now A153 road to the south of the village. A siding over half-a-mile long was laid from a point just west of the level-crossing to the west of Honington Station. It then made a right angled turn, crossing the A153 on the level at its junction with the A607. At its eastern end it ran under a tipping stage to which the quarry's 3' gauge tramway ran. This tramway, worked by horses, eventually extended for about one mile and its trucks were loaded by hand. The workings closed in 1921 after the best quality stone had been removed.

The only evidence today is around the A153/A607 road junction: small woods on either side have a central gap and through this gap once rumbled trainloads of iron ore; indeed, level-crossing gates remained here until the early 1950s.

(e) *Leadenham*

The ironstone was found to outcrop at the top of the Lincolnshire Edge escarpment, as well as at its foot, but in only

Figure 17.4   *The route of the siding serving Honington Quarry ran through this gap in the trees, at the A607/A153 junction*   © Author

one location south of Lincoln was it exploited, at Leadenham.

The quarry was first worked in about 1890 by Major George Dove. To reach it an exchange-siding was laid from the east side of Leadenham Station, northwards along the eastern side of the A607 on an embankment. The line then reversed at this embankment and ran southwards across the fields to the foot of the escarpment. (*See* Figure 17.5.) The total length of railway was about three quarters of a mile. At its end a 2' 6" gauge cable-incline, one third of a mile long, came down the hillside to a tipping stage alongside the minor road running from the village to Leadenham Heath. This tramway extended into the quarry itself.

The method of working was that stone was loaded into narrow-gauge quarry trucks which were pulled by horses to the incline. Six loaded wagons at a time, balanced by six empties removed. Limestone had also been quarried here, and it was for this that it was reopened in 1942 by the Leadenham Stone Company Limited, to help meet a demand caused by the construction of local airfields.

The major remnant which can be seen today is the embankment, now tree-covered, alongside the A607. It is now pierced by the main entrance to the William Robertson School. In the centre of the fields to the east of Leadenham Station is a small wood, through the centre of which the siding ran, and in the autumn, after ploughing, the route up to this wood is discernible as a dark soil mark.

Figure 17.5   *The hillside east of Leadenham Station with the route of the line to the tipping stage picked out. This ran through the centre of the trees in the middle of the photograph. The route of the cable-incline, at right angles running down the hillside from the quarry hidden behind the trees on the crest, is also shown*   © Author

Figure 17.6   *The tree-covered embankment alongside the A607 outside the William Robertson School, north of Leadenham railway bridge. This was the site of the siding serving the quarry on the hilltop at Leadenham*   © Author

going up, were lowered down to the tipping stage over the standard gauge trucks. Loaded trucks, again horse-hauled, were taken down to the exchange-siding to be collected by the Great Northern Railway daily. The ore was sent to Lysaght's Works at Scunthorpe via Lincoln.

After 1920 the quarry was worked by the Barnstone Blue Lias Lime Company. The working ceased in 1925 because of increasing overburden, and the incline and sidings were then

18

Lincoln to Boston

The history of the Lincoln to Boston line is closely bound up with the River Witham, on whose bank the railway was built for most of its route.

It was opened, double-track throughout, on 17 October 1848, as part of the Great Northern Railway's Lincolnshire Loop Line, this 37-mile stretch forming the majority of the 58-mile route from Werrington Junction, north of Peterborough, to Lincoln. Until the opening of the 'Towns' line, from Peterborough to Doncaster, in 1852, it was the route taken by the main-line trains from London to the north.

Stations were provided at Washingborough, Five Mile House, Bardney, Southrey, Stixwould, Kirkstead (renamed Woodhall Junction on 10 July 1922), Tattershall, Dogdyke and Langrick. These were communities on, or close to, the riverbank, served by packet boats and, except Tattershall where there was a bridge, at places where ferries crossed the river. The oddly

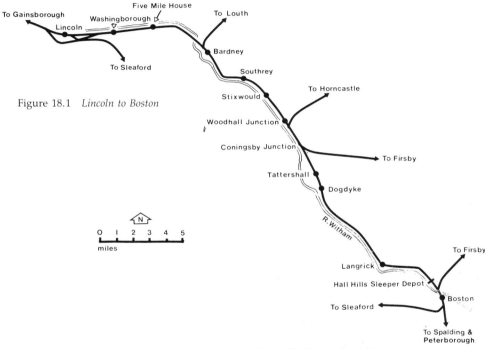

Figure 18.1   *Lincoln to Boston*

Figure 18.2   *Washingborough Junction in the early 1950s. The line to the right, on which waits a Lincoln–Boston goods train with a J6 0–6–0 at its head, was part of the Lincolnshire Loop Line, opened in 1848. A Skegness bound passenger train with a K2 2–6–0, is coming down the short section of line from Greetwell Junction on the former Great Northern and Great Eastern Joint Railway. By using this route Loop Line trains which were not due to stop at Lincoln Central – goods and excursion traffic – could gain the Lincoln Avoiding Line, built to keep such traffic away from the city's central area level-crossings. The line to the right was closed following track reorganisation in Lincoln as a result of a derailment east of Lincoln Central on 2 June 1962. An express sleeping car train from Kings Cross to Edinburgh, diverted because of main line engineering work, took a sharp curve with a 15 mph speed restriction at 50 mph and seven coaches left the track. Three people were killed and fifty injured. This was Lincoln's worst rail disaster*   © G Flatters

named Five Mile House served Fiskerton village but was, not surprisingly, five miles from Lincoln Central Station. The railway eventually killed off the steam packets, although they lingered on for a number of years, finally ending about 1860.

Additional traffic was brought to the line in 1855 with the

Figure 18.3   The ferry over the River Witham at Five Mile House. The station was built to serve Fiskerton village on the north bank and travellers used the ferry to reach the trains. This was a typical feature of most of the Loop Line stations, particularly in their early days. They also served as unofficial diving platforms on hot summer days – an activity that would be frowned on nowadays!   © E Steele

Figure 18.4   RCTS Railtour on 16 May 1954 at Bardney. The engine is No 64199, a Gresley J6 0–6–0 which then took this train to Louth via Donington on Bain

© E Neve

opening of the Horncastle Branch, in 1874 when the Bardney–Louth Line was opened, and in 1913 with the construction of the 'New' Line from Coningsby Junction to Boston.

In 1900 the Great Northern opened their sleeper depot at Hall Hills, north of Boston. Timber for sleepers was imported through Boston, and they were produced here. The depot had its own 2' 6" gauge tramway, and its own standard-gauge departmental locomotive. During the final years of the GNR's separate existence an old 0–6–0 saddle tank engine No 470 was used. This dated from 1872 when it had been rebuilt with a few components taken from a Manning Wardle 0–6–0 tank originally built for the West Yorkshire Railway in 1867. No 470 received the suffix 'A' in 1919 and remained in use at Boston until replaced by Sentinel 0–4–0 No 4801, Class Y1, in 1926. In the 1950s the depot engine was a Sentinel 0–4–0 tank, Class Y3, No 7, formerly BR 68166.

Because of its various connections, the railway provided a good service to the variety of communities in its area. Apart from Dogdyke on the west bank of the river, all the stations served villages on the north and east bank. These ranged in size from the small town of Woodhall Spa to the tiny villages of Southrey and Stixwould. On the opposite bank, fenland hamlets and scattered farms were numerous. In 1938 there were eleven passenger trains each way daily between Lincoln and Boston, one each way from Lincoln to Skegness, one from Boston to Woodhall, and one early morning workman's train from Lincoln to Bardney. In addition, Bardney had five trains each way to and from Louth and Woodhall Junction had six each way to Firsby and Skegness and eight each way to Horn-

Figure 18.6   *A view of Tattershall Station in the early 1930s*   Courtesy P Carter

castle. The fare for the workman's special at Bardney was 6½d (2½p) return, and a cheap day-return to Lincoln was 9½d (4p). For 1s 6d (7½p) villagers could take an evening excursion to Skegness, leaving at 5 pm and returning at midnight. In the 1950s the branch was amongst the first in the area to be dieselised on the introduction of diesel multiple unit trains.

In the summer season, the traffic was greatly augmented by excursion traffic to the coast, and by fisherman's specials. In fact, in the early 1950s there could be sixty trains a day on summer Saturdays, including the regular services. Indeed, it was principally to carry the regular, heavy coastal-excursion traffic that the 'New' line to Bellwater Junction had been built, to avoid a reversal at Boston and give shorter journey times to Mablethorpe and Skegness. (*See* Chapter 20.)

The rivers of Lincolnshire have always provided some of the best coarse fishing in the country, and one of the principal rivers for this is the River Witham. This fact was exploited and weekend fishing specials became an important source of revenue. Just before the Second World War, two Saturday and

Figure 18.5   *Woodhall Junction in 1928. Standing near the signal box is a brand new Clayton railcar No 2130,* Bang Up, *on trial. Eleven of these were built by Claytons in Lincoln, all named after former horse-drawn mail coaches. They were given a colourful livery of green and cream but were not a success. The railwayman's verdict on* Bang Up *was that it was 'a poor thing'*

Courtesy Stephenson Locomotive Society

Figure 18.7 *A train on its way to Lincoln pauses at Stixwould Station in August 1970, two months before the passenger service was lost. Stixwould was typical of the smaller stations on the line, with a single-storey booking office and waiting room on one platform. The Stationmaster's house was a detached building on the opposite side of the road. The level-crossing gave access to the river bank, where in earlier years the ferry operating under the Stationmaster's supervision was large enough to carry one car over the River Witham to Blankney Fen. This was the site of an incident in 1951 when a motorist, driving onto the ferry before it was lined up properly with the bank went straight into the river* © P Grey

four Sunday specials from Sheffield and Rotherham, each consisting of twelve coaches, would stop at all stations. This traffic ceased in the mid 1960s.

In common with most other rural lines, the Lincoln to Boston had quite heavy freight traffic for much of its life, and sidings were busy with trucks loading and unloading agricultural produce and various commodities for the local shops and businesses. Much of the area was poorly served by roads, and although bridges were built at Langrick, Kirkstead and Bardney, to replace their ferries, the others remained in use, latterly for pedestrians only. An interesting aspect of this is that responsibility for the ferry operation lay with stationmasters. Additional traffic came to the line in the inter-war period, when a private siding was provided for Morrell's Canning Factory at Bardney, and the Bardney Sugar Beet Factory, with its own internal railway system, opened in 1927.

The first stations to lose both passenger and goods services were Washingborough, from 29 July 1940, and Five Mile House,

Figure 18.8 *A 04 Class, 2–8–0 No 63787 at Bardney, about 1960. It had probably just delivered a train of coal to the sugar-beet factory as at this time its home shed was Stavely, near Chesterfield. Built in 1917 for the Railway Operating Division, it was taken into LNER stock in 1924* © Glenn Answer

Tattershall were closed completely. As a substitute, three extra trains between Lincoln and Boston via Sleaford were provided. Hall Hills Depot remained rail-served from Boston for another eighteen months before it too closed. The northern part of the branch remained served by trains from Lincoln to either Coningsby or Tumby Woodside, where they terminated, and to Firsby and Skegness. These services were lost from 5 October 1970 along with services over much of the East Lincolnshire Main Line, and Southrey and Stixwould Stations closed completely.

Goods traffic remained, to Bardney for the Sugar Beet Factory, and to Woodhall Junction, to give access to the Horncastle Branch. This latter traffic ceased from 5 April 1971, when Horncastle and Woodhall Junction goods yards were closed, and

Figure 18.9 *Coningsby Junction signal box in the summer of 1971, after eight years of disuse. The track to Boston had long disappeared, apart from this obsolete crossover. It was at a very isolated spot, over a mile from the nearest road, but even so, it appeared to have suffered at the hands of the vandals* © Author

Figure 18.10 *Southrey Station in July 1971 – the line was completely closed at this time. The Stationmaster's house can be seen in the background – today its garage displays one of the signal box nameboards; the platforms and concrete station nameboards, still survive* © Author

from 15 September 1958. At the latter, however, anglers' trains continued to call at summer weekends until September 1964. The goods yard at Southrey closed on 1 October 1955, that at Stixwould on 17 June 1963, and the goods yard at Bardney closed for other than private sidings' traffic on 3 May 1965.

In 1963, following the revelation that £72 000 expenditure was required on signals and trackwork which traffic levels could not justify, the closure of the fourteen miles between Coningsby Junction and Boston was announced. This took effect from 17 June that year, and the stations at Langrick, Dogdyke and

Figure 18.11 *The British Sugar Corporation had extensive sidings at their Bardney factory and always employed their own locomotive to move wagons around the works. Here, the last one, this Ruston shunter, built in Lincoln, pauses in its work on 8 December 1972. In the background is the former Bardney Station goods shed, a standard Great Northern design to be seen at many of its Lincolnshire stations*
© Author

only the line to Bardney remained. This was then worked as a private siding, bringing in coal during the winter, and taking out beet pulp at other times for destinations countrywide. Trains ran as required. In January 1981 the British Sugar Corporation dispensed with rail traffic and the last vestige of the branch was lifted; but before this the line had performed one last duty – a royal duty: the train carrying the Queen and the Duke of

Figure 18.12 *On 21 January 1981, a special train enters Bardney Station over the level-crossing immediately prior to the closure of what was by then the last vestige of the line, a private siding seven-miles-long serving the Bardney Sugar-Beet Factory. This was the very last passenger train to use the branch, although the track remained for another two years*
© Lincolnshire Echo

Edinburgh for their visit to Lincoln on 14 November 1980 was stabled for the previous night at the site of Five Mile House Station.

There is, however, a very interesting rare survival of this line: the cast-iron Victorian Gentlemen's Toilet, dating from about 1880, which graced the down platform can now be seen (but not used!), at the Museum of Lincolnshire Life, in Lincoln.

It seems strange to reflect that the quiet villages and hamlets along the riverside, only some of which see an occasional market-day bus today, enjoyed regular reliable daily public transport for two hundred years, first by boat and later by train. Is this really progress?

Figure 18.13   Woodhall Junction Station in July 1971. The photograph shows the up and down platforms. The Horncastle Branch platform was the opposite face of the up platform, off to the left of the photograph. The wooden waiting rooms on the down platform were still signposted as 'Waiting Room' and 'Ladies Waiting Room', a reminder of the provision of separate facilities for ladies and their children at most stations. Just disappearing into the undergrowth to the left of this building is the station's unique feature, an ornate cast-iron Victorian 'gents" toilet. Made in Glasgow in 1880, it was rescued and re-erected at the Museum of Lincolnshire Life in Lincoln. A similar one survives alongside the SS Great Britain *in Bristol Docks*   © Author

19

The Horncastle Branch

Looking at the remains of this branch line today it is difficult to imagine how busy it once was, passing as it does through isolated rural countryside. But at one time the two small towns it served bustled with activity, an activity encouraged and enhanced by their railway service.

Woodhall Spa grew from a tiny hamlet to a fashionable spa town after drilling operations to discover coal in 1811 found only water. This water was found to have healing powers and taking the water became *de rigeur* for Edwardian society. As a contrast, Horncastle became one of the most important centres in the country for the buying and selling of horses.

The Horncastle and Kirkstead Junction Railway Company opened their 7½-mile single-track line from the Great Northern Railways (GNR) at Kirkstead on 11 August 1855. The line was worked by the GNR from the beginning although the Company remained independent until 1923. Stations were at Woodhall Spa and Horncastle. Kirkstead was renamed Woodhall Junction on 10 July 1922.

A bath-house at Woodhall Spa was built in 1836 but the number of visitors was restricted because of the lack of suitable transport links. The opening of the Lincolnshire Loop Line

Figure 19.2 *Horncastle terminus on a snowy day, 3 January 1968. The goods yard crane did not survive for much longer after this date. There were really two yards here; this one had a private siding to a warehouse, out of sight on the right, and once a wagon turntable gave access to the doors in the building on the left. Further sidings, including the oil depot which kept the line open for so long, were behind the station buildings, at a lower level* © Author

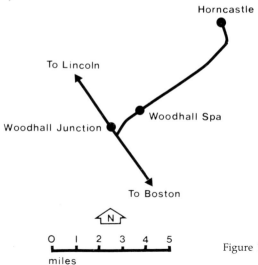

Figure 19.1 *The Horncastle Branch*

town, there was no room for more and so the siding was laid alongside the line, west of the Tattershall Road level-crossing and wagons had to be collected and delivered by freight trains on their return journey from the terminus. Moreover, because the junction with the GNR faced away from Kirkstead, trains had to reverse out of the station before setting out to Horncastle.

In 1887 there were eight trains each way daily, taking twenty-eight minutes for the journey, with extra trains on Monday, Tuesday, Thursday and Saturday and from 1898 one included a through-coach from Kings Cross. The Sunday service was

Figure 19.3 *In the summer of 1970 a goods train bound for Lincoln via Woodhall Junction crosses Coningsby Road level-crossing in Woodhall Spa. This was the site of the one siding that the town boasted* © Richard Goodman

Figure 19.4 *Woodhall Spa Station in 1952, two years before closure. Built on a very constricted site, there was room only for two platforms and a passing loop. The signal box was also on the platform and can just be seen beyond the awning on the left-hand platform* Courtesy M White Collection

from Boston to Lincoln in 1848, and the construction of the Horncastle Branch gave great impetus to the development of the town. In 1841 the population was only 280. With the railway came new hotels, guest-houses, pleasure-grounds, schools, churches and houses. Between 1886 and 1911 the population increased five-fold.

At Horncastle there were extensive goods sidings and in 1874 the goods shed here was enlarged and the station platform lengthened. Woodhall Spa had no siding until one was opened on 4 April 1887. The line was very constricted through the discontinued in June 1868. By 1910 the basic service had fallen to six each way with additional market-day services, but by 1938 it had risen again to eight with one additional service on Saturdays.

The Autumn Horncastle Horse Fairs were renowned for the quality of the animals being sold, and the railway provided the means for local horses to be brought in, and despatched to their new owners at destinations countrywide. The late 1800s were the peak years and up to 150 horses a day would arrive at the station for several days before. As the sales progressed, up to five special trains a day would take sixty horses at a time away from the town, and up to thirty extra station staff would be

Figure 19.5 The articulated twin set of coaches of Great Northern origin used on the Branch trains in its final years. They were standing in the bay platform at Horncastle Station
                                                                              © R K McKenny

Figure 19.6 *A week before closure, a train on its way to Woodhall Spa is about to pass under the only overbridge on the line, carrying the Woodhall Spa to Horncastle Road*
                                                                              © Author

drafted in, to augment the usual eighteen staff, to deal with them. From the 1890s the size of the fair gradually fell up to the time of the First World War, and after a brief, big revival of demand, especially from the Army, the trade petered out after 1918 as the use of mechanical transport increased. For a time during the Second World War further horse specials ran, meeting a new demand when petrol was scarce. Regular traffic was mainly agricultural produce, oil and parcels. Horncastle was the principal market town for a large rural area, and in the late 1940s seventeen lorries were used by the London and North Eastern Railway (LNER) for the collection and delivery of railway goods.

A single-road engine shed was provided at Horncastle until 1924 to house the branch engine worked by a local crew. In

LNER days an engine from Lincoln worked to Horncastle with a goods train at 6.45 am, afterwards covering branch passenger duties until returning to Lincoln with the 7.40 pm goods train. Boston sent a Class C12 4–4–2T with empty coaches to Horncastle to run one return trip to Woodhall Junction and the 9.10 am to Boston which included the through London coach when operating. A second Boston engine, 0–6–0 tender, took a goods train to Lincoln, and then ran back light to Woodhall Junction for the 4.10 pm passenger to Horncastle and back with the 4.45 pm. This engine then took the 5.20 pm goods to Boston. The C12 again worked to Horncastle with the 6.33 pm from Boston conveying the through coach off the 4.0 pm from Kings Cross, afterwards returning light to Boston.

The line's passenger service was an early casualty, trains ceasing to run from 13 September 1954 – the level of traffic could not justify the expenditure. However, a single goods train ran daily for another seventeen years. Final closure came on 5 April 1971, and for six months prior to that, after the passenger services on the line from Lincoln to Coningsby stopped, Horncastle goods trains were the only users of the former Loop Line between Bardney and Woodhall Junction.

The trackbed remains, and much of it has been incorporated into the Viking Way long-distance footpath. Users can now view the countryside at a much more sedate pace than did our grandparents.

Figure 19.7   *The last Horncastle Branch goods train on Saturday 3 April 1971, pictured here at Woodhall Junction*   © *Lincolnshire Echo*

Coningsby Junction to Bellwater Junction

The year was 1917, and for over two years the young men of Europe had beem embroiled on the Western Front. Tommy was called to the colours and drafted to France. Alas he was never to return; in fact he did not reach the other side of the Channel as his ship was sunk on the way and his fate was that of the sailor's grave.

Nothing out of the ordinary in those troubled times, but in this case there was, as this Tommy was a single line of railway track, fifteen miles long. The desperate need for good communications in France led to one track of the route from Coningsby

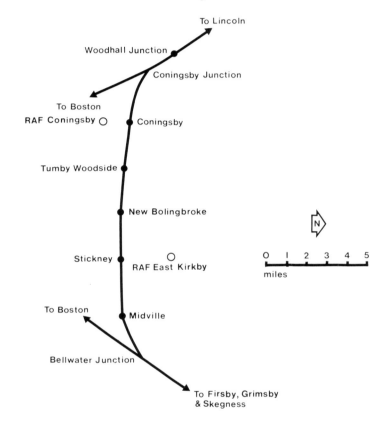

Figure 20.2 *Coningsby Junction to Bellwater Junction*

Junction to Bellwater Junction being lifted, but it never reached its destination.

The growth of the day trip and holiday trade for the Great Northern Railway (GNR) is charted in Chapter 10. From the

Figure 20.1 *Railway routes to the Lincolnshire Coast*

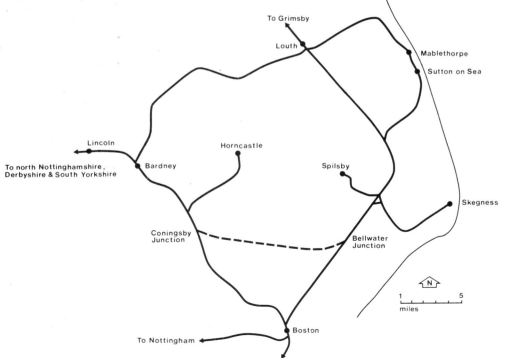

1870s excursion traffic to the Lincolnshire coastal resorts of Skegness, Mablethorpe and Sutton on Sea from cities and towns as diverse as London, Nottingham, Derby, Sheffield, Leeds and Bradford became increasingly important. Trains from London and Nottingham could run direct to the holiday towns, but those from further north faced indirect routes, via Lincoln and Boston, reversing at Boston, or via Lincoln, Bardney and Louth, reversing at Bardney and again at Louth. From as early as 1884 the GNR were looking at ways to shorten the route and speed the journey. This line was the result, serving the rural area through which it passed as well as carrying the excursion trains from the North Midlands and South Yorkshire. It cut ten miles off the former journey from Lincoln, via Boston.

It was the last of the major routes to be built in Lincolnshire, and it opened on 1 July 1913. The double line of rails fifteen miles long, served stations at Coningsby, Tumby Woodside, New Bolingbroke, Stickney and Midville. Local traffic was always slight, usually four trains each way daily between

Figure 20.4   New Bolingbroke Station, pictured in 1971. New Bolingbroke village was an early nineteenth century attempt to found a new town, which was largely a failure. It was to remain a small village, but of sufficient size to warrant the building of this station in due course, when the railway came   © Author

Figure 20.3   The interior of Tumby Woodside signal box after closure. The instruments and many other small items recoverable by so-called railway enthusiasts were swiftly removed by British Rail   © Author

much extra traffic to the stations at Coningsby and Stickney. At Stickney, where the goods yard was permanently busy, the staff maintained that they knew how many bombers had not returned from the previous night's raid by counting the number of replacement aircrew arriving there on the 1.00 pm train.

An increase in the number of trains on the line came after the closure in June 1963 of part of the Lincolnshire Loop Line, between Coningsby Junction and Boston, and Coningsby served as the railhead for the areas previously catered for by Tattershall and Dogdyke Stations (*see* Chapter 18), and became

Figure 20.5   The booking office and signal box at Midville Station in the summer of 1971. The design of the stations at Southrey and Stixwould on the Lincoln–Boston Line were very similar to this   © Author

Figure 20.6   The nature of the flat fenland countryside traversed by the line is well illustrated here. The view westwards from Midville with its overgrown refuge siding was taken on 19 January 1971, three months after closure. The only real evidence of this, however, is that the signal arm has been removed   © Author

Lincoln and Skegness. It was immediately dubbed 'The New Line' by railwaymen, and so it remained for all its life.

However, two years after its opening it was temporarily closed as part of the railway's effort to reduce their consumption of coal. Relaying of the missing track began in June 1922, and the line reopened the following year.

In its heyday, Tumby Woodside and Coningsby were its most important stations – train loads of Lincolnshire potatoes grown in the fertile fen soil regularly left Tumby Woodside in the season. In the Second World War bomber airfields were opened, at Coningsby in 1941, and at East Kirkby in 1943, bringing for three trains each way daily from Lincoln, the remainder of the branch served only by four Lincoln to Firsby trains, and three in the opposite direction.

On 5 October 1970 the end came for the route between Coningsby and Bellwater Junction, along with many miles of other Lincolnshire line. Removal of the track was completed by May 1972 and little now remains of this once busy route.

Figure 20.7 *A Firsby train calls at Stickney Station in the summer of 1970. The platforms and track are already becoming grass-grown, foretelling the closure that was soon to come. It was here, that, during the Second World War, the staff could tell how many Lancasters had been lost from East Kirkby airfield in recent raids by noting the number of replacement aircrew arriving* © M Hall

Figure 20.8 *On 9 August 1970, Coningsby's tidy station basks in the summer sun* © P Grey

the terminus for some Lincoln trains. But this glory was short lived: from 7 October 1968, as an economy measure, the stations became unstaffed halts, tickets being issued on the train by conductor guards. By 1970, Tumby Woodside was the terminus

21

The Spilsby Branch

Adolf Hitler has been blamed for many things. He could also be blamed for bringing to an end the passenger service on this branch, as in 1939 it was one of several scheduled to be closed countrywide as an economy measure in the event of war. Accordingly, the service was suspended on 10 September 1939, and was never reinstated. Goods traffic, however, ran for another nineteen years.

The four-and-a-half-mile, single-track branch had been opened on Friday 1 May 1868. The town was decked with flags, the church bells rang and a public luncheon was held in the Corn Exchange on the day the first train left Spilsby Station. There was a small engine shed at the terminus and one inter-

Figure 21.1   *The Spilsby Branch*

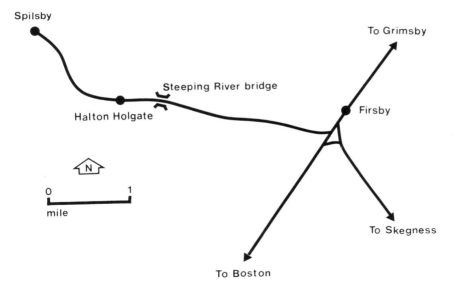

Figure 21.2   *Boston J6, 0–6–0, No 64260 arrives at Spilsby on 8 November 1958. Although the line was to close three weeks hence the train comprises a respectable ten wagons plus guards van*   Courtesy M White Collection

mediate station, at Halton Holgate, where the train would stop on request. The line was built by the Spilsby and Firsby Railway Company and worked by the Great Northern Railway who provided an engine and rolling stock, and on 1 January 1891 they took over the line. There was, for most of its life, a basic service of seven passenger trains a day each way, taking fifteen minutes for the single journey.

In 1886 a proposal was made for a Lincoln, Horncastle, Spilsby and East Coast Railway, to link the county town with

90

Figure 21.3   *A week before final closure, the branch goods train, with J6, 0–6–0, No 64214 at its head, pauses at Halton Holgate on its way to Spilsby*   © H Davies

the seaside resorts of Skegness and Mablethorpe. This would have required a new line linking the Horncastle and Spilsby terminal stations, over the Lincolnshire Wolds, together with spurs elsewhere to allow through-running on other lines already built. There was little support, and the project was abandoned in 1891.

Half-a-mile east of Halton Holgate the line crossed the Steeping River, immortalised in literature as *The Brook* in Tennyson's famous poem of that title. By 1958 the state of the bridge had become so poor that it was considered beyond repair. Despite local opposition, British Railways decided that it could not justify the cost of building a new bridge and the line must therefore close. The last train ran on 30 November 1958 and the river bridge was then removed. Tennyson's brook might say today 'Railways may come and railways may go, but I go on for ever'.

Figure 21.4 *The disused Spilsby Station, with no track, in the early 1960s. The building was demolished in 1965* © Richard Goodman

92

22

The Cranwell Branch

The Cranwell Branch was built by the Admiralty, even though its terminus was twenty-five miles from the sea. In 1916 the Royal Naval Air Service opened an airfield, which they named *HMS Daedalus*, for aircraft and airships, on the heathland two miles west of Cranwell village. For its construction the contractor had built a line from Sleaford, laid on the existing ground with no earthworks, but the bad winter of 1915–16 proved that a permanent and reliable means of moving stores and equipment was needed.

Three routes were considered, one, from Caythorpe Station – this was ruled out because of the climb up the hillside from there; two, from Ancaster – it was deemed that suitable space

Figure 22.1 *The Cranwell Branch*

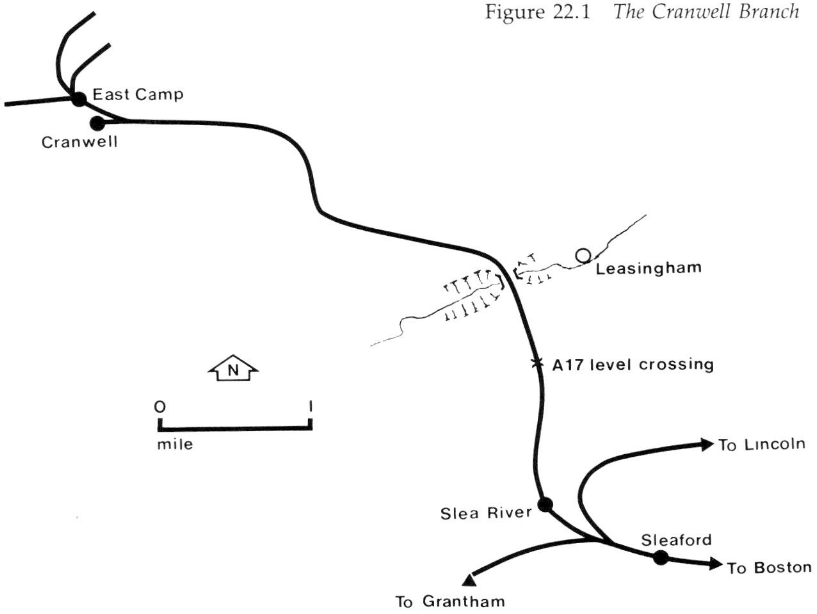

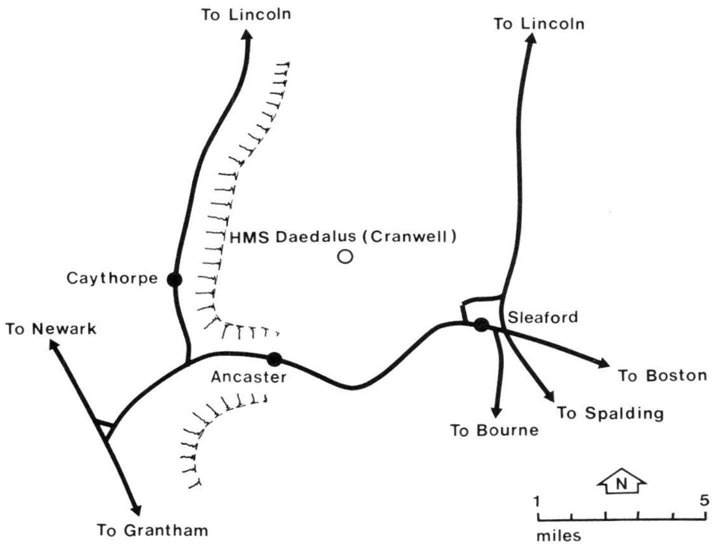

Figure 22.2 *Railway routes in the Cranwell area, 1916*

for exchange sidings could not be found here; and three, along the line of the contractor's railway – this route was chosen.

The line was built under Great Northern Railway (GNR) supervision, the 5¼ miles of single track opening in 1917. There were a number of steep gradients, two of 1 in 50 leaving Slea River Platform before the A17 level-crossing was reached, and 1 in 50 down on either side of a small valley to the west of Leasingham village. In the early days the A17 level-crossing was operated by a gateman, but for most of the life of the crossing this was a job for the train crew.

The Royal Air Force was formed on 1 April 1918, by merging

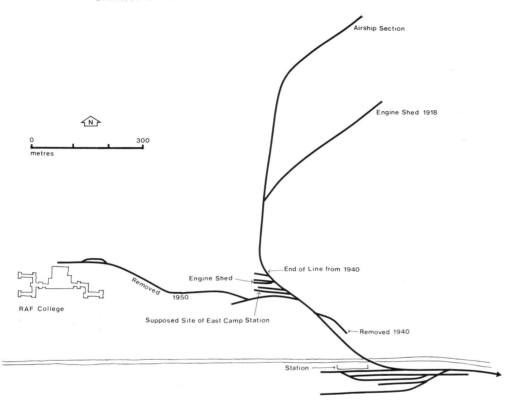

Figure 22.3 *Railway lines at RAF Cranwell*

road; it is now the Station Guardroom. There were halts – simple line-side platforms – at East Camp, north of the main station, and at Slea River, half a mile north of the junction with the GNR at Sleaford, from where a river-bank footpath led to the town, half a mile away. Goods facilities provided were exchange-sidings with the GNR adjacent to Sleaford west box, and a variety of depots and sidings serving various parts of the camp.

Prior to 1918 five of the contractor's 0–6–0 Manning Wardle tank engines were retained to work the line. Early in 1918 these were replaced with two locomotives from Devonport Dockyard, numbered 1 and 2. Both were built by Manning Wardle. No 2, Works No 1930, was built in 1917, and subsequently sold to a Nottinghamshire colliery in 1926. No 1 was of an earlier date, and was sold for scrap in 1925.

Figure 22.4 *A 0–6–0 tank, No 129, built by Hudswell Clarke and Co of Leeds. Delivered new to the line in November 1924, it is shown here in 1953 taking water before hauling a morning goods train to Sleaford*

Courtesy College Library, RAF Cranwell

the Royal Naval Air Service and the Royal Flying Corps. Cranwell Camp, and its railway, became the property of the RAF from that date. This ended certain naval traditions at Cranwell, common to other 'stone frigates': the Dining Hall had been the 'messdeck', the cookhouse the 'galley', and 'going ashore in the liberty boat' referred to taking the 'Cranwell Express' to Sleaford.

There were three passenger stations of which the main one was the terminus, in the centre of the camp, alongside the main

Figure 22.5   *A Peckett 0–4–0, AMWD No 127, built in 1918 and transferred to Cranwell in 1925, seen here at Cranwell in May 1953. Note the sack of coal on the buffer beam, carried in case the limited bunker was insufficient on any journey*
Courtesy College Library, RAF Cranwell

These engines were replaced in 1924 with an 0–6–0 tank purchased new from Hudswell Clarke of Leeds, numbered 129, (Works No 1541), and in 1925 with a Peckett 0–4–0 saddle tank, numbered 127, (Works No 1521), built in 1918 and transferred from Cardington. Both these worked on the line for many years, 129 being the last in use before being sold into NCB ownership at Fishburn Colliery, Durham, in 1957.

Two diesel locomotives were also tried out. One, a Fowler, built in 1939, transferred here from Heywood about 1951; of the other no details are known. Both were soon transferred to Cardington, proving unequal to the task the gradients imposed with loaded trains.

Although built primarily for freight, from its early days the line had a passenger service. There were thirteen four-wheeled

and six-wheeled passenger coaches, bought secondhand from the GNR before 1919. They had been built at the turn of the century for the Metropolitan Service between New Barnet and Moorgate, their Lincolnshire home being a stark contrast to their previous one. Eight coaches were usually sufficient on any train except on Saturdays when all thirteen were often used. The Third Class return fare was threepence (1¼p).

Normally seven return journeys would be made daily, taking fifteen to twenty minutes for the single journey. All but one ran to Sleaford Station. The exception was a mixed train which left its passengers at Slea River, collected wagons from the sidings, then waited at Slea River before making the return journey. There was an additional daily train for freight only. Bus competition brought the regular passenger trains to an end in 1927.

Figure 22.6   *At Cranwell, on 19 July 1949, the Fowler diesel collided with a baby Austin on a level-crossing near East Camp. There were no injuries. The use of a diesel locomotive was a short-lived experiment as the loads were too heavy for them on this steeply graded line*   Courtesy College Library, RAF Cranwell

Figure 22.7 *A Coronation Special, with J6 0–6–0 No 64196, at Cranwell Station platform. On special occasions, for longer, heavier trains these engines would use the branch. Another locomotive is at the rear of this thirteen coach train, and the sharp drop in gradient at the east end of the station can clearly be noted*
Courtesy College Library, RAF Cranwell

Special-leave trains for RAF personnel ran from Sleaford to Kings Cross via Grantham. For example, on 20 December 1921 a thirteen coach train headed by C1 Atlantic No 1441, followed by another C1 No 301 on fourteen coaches reached London just before 2.0 pm. On 22 December 1922, two eleven-coach specials were hauled by 4–4–0s Nos 59 and 1374. Return specials on 5 January 1923 started from Kings Cross at 3.40 and 4.0 pm in charge of *Klondyke* 4–4–2 No 257 and large Atlantic No 1430 respectively. Occasionally such specials would traverse the branch from Sleaford, but the accommodation and layout at the terminus placed severe restrictions on their number and length.

Other special trains ran from time to time. The Crusaders' Union, a boys' organisation, visited Cranwell on two occasions. On Thursday 16 April 1931 the first of these started from Kings Cross at 9.50 am, the thirteen-coach train included four kitchen cars and weighed a total of 520 tons. It was hauled to Sleaford by A1 Pacific No 2552, *Sansovino*. The passengers transferred at Sleaford to twelve six-wheeled coaches supplied from Boston, together with an 0–6–0 locomotive, for the journey over the camp lines. The special train returned to London from Sleaford behind another A1, No 2560 *Pretty Polly*. On the second occasion in April 1938 the train was hauled both ways between London and Grantham by A4 Pacific No 4498 *Sir Nigel Gresley*.

There were rarely more than two goods trains a day, and later in the life of the line, one a day sufficed, the engine never venturing onto British Railways' metals; the end came in August 1956 when the line closed. The rails were removed the following year and now few traces of it remain.

23

Belton Park Military Railway

Few records are available, and few photographs appear to have survived of this, the least known and least documented of all the county's railways. With the sole exception of the Alford and Sutton Tramway it was Lincolnshire's shortest-lived railway.

During the First World War part of Belton Park, on the northern outskirts of Grantham, was turned into a vast Army camp, becoming the base of the Machine Gun Corps. The camp grew to cover many acres, to provide a temporary home for thousands of soldiers, and to be the destination and point of despatch for tons of domestic and military supplies.

At first the railhead was Grantham Station, but this was deemed to be inconvenient, being about four miles distant, so, in 1916, a single-track railway line, four-and-a-half-miles long, was built to serve it.

The junction was with the East Coast Main Line, at a point half-a-mile south of Peascliff Tunnel where a signal box was built. This gave access to the branch, and to two exchange-sidings. The line then crossed the Great Gonerby to Manthorpe road, Belton Lane, on the level, turning immediately to run parallel to it, almost alongside. It then crossed what is now the A607 and entered Belton Park. Here the River Witham lies in a small valley, and to reach the bottom, and cross the river, reversal was necessary. There was no run-round loop, and so trains were propelled in one direction away from it. The bridge over the river was rather low, and at times covered with flood water, but this did not prevent trains running at such times. Trains then skirted the southern edge of Belton Park to reach a small single-road engine shed, sited near to the present day Golf Clubhouse. Here the line divided, one arm running north-west, serving a number of dispersed sidings, the other south and east, into what are now a number of housing estates, and crossing Harrowby Lane to serve a military hospital. There is

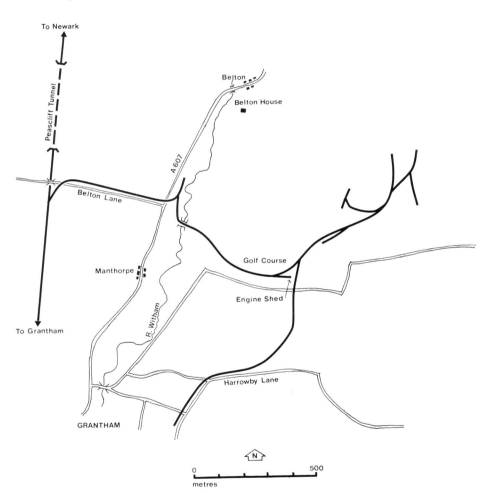

Figure 23.1 *Belton Park Military Railway*

1293), of 1895, numbered 91 in War Department stock. For a short time after closure of the line it worked at RAF Cranwell before being transferred to Catterick Camp.

With the end of the war the camp was no longer needed and was progressively run down. The line was removed in 1924, and no trace remains of it today.

Figure 23.2   *The site of the junction with the East Coast Main Line, half-a-mile south of Peascliff Tunnel. This view is looking south; the junction was at the point on the far side of the line where the wall of the cutting peters out. The branch then crossed the field on the left-hand side of the photograph, its route being where the darker soil can be seen*   © Author

Figure 23.3   *Manning Wardle 0–4–0 saddle tank, War Department No 91, with a small short train heading for the main line and its exchange-sidings. The photograph was taken in the Park, probably near to the engine shed*   © Richard Tarpey

no record of any signalling, but as only one engine was recorded it was probably unnecessary.

The line was worked by one War Department 0–4–0 shunting engine which made a daily return trip to either the exchange-sidings, or, on occasions, to Grantham goods yard, for wagons only. Troops continued to march to and from Grantham Station by road. The engine was a Manning Wardle, (works number

24

The Denton and Harlaxton Ironstone Railways

Ironstone was first quarried in the Woolsthorpe area in about 1879, with the stone being taken by horse and cart to Woolsthorpe Wharf on the Grantham Canal. Output was limited because of the transport involved, and so in 1883 the Great Northern Railway (GNR) opened a branch from Belvoir Junction on their Grantham to Nottingham Line, three miles to Woolsthorpe Wharf, and from 3 August 1885 stone was taken out by train. The workings were on the hilltop above the canal side; sidings and a 3' gauge tramway with a cable-incline were constructed to a tipping stage from Brewer's Grave. This quarry was closed in 1918.

Ironstone was quarried in Harston Parish in 1885 by the Stanton Ironworks Company, and the GNR Branch was extended another two miles to Denton Sidings in that year. The company also provided two agricultural sidings, Denton and Welbys, to generate additional traffic. Horse and cart transport of ore soon gave way to a 3' gauge tramway, which was successively extended, especially after 1918. The private tramway was extended as new quarries were opened, to Knipton Pit in 1920 and subsequently on to a point west of Croxton Kerrial, a total of three miles away from Denton Sidings. These tramways were converted to the standard gauge in 1948.

From 1916 to 1930, the workings were extended into Denton Park, requiring another mile of tramway from a junction alongside the Denton–Harston Road. It was converted to standard gauge in 1950. It was at this junction that Stanton Ironworks established a small workshop for engine maintenance.

The demand for iron and steel during World War Two was so great that the Stanton Ironworks Co Ltd built a new four-mile length from Casthorpe Junction on the original line, on to the hillside above Harlaxton to tap additional workable stone.

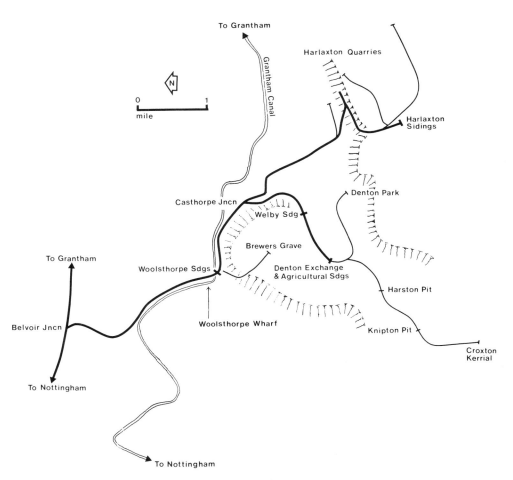

Figure 24.1 *The Denton and Harlaxton ironstone railways*

99

In 1897 there were five trains despatched daily to Colwick on the outskirts of Nottingham. One of these from Denton, the others from Woolsthorpe. Two trains only ran on Saturdays, both from Denton, picking up at Woolsthorpe.

During the Second World War there were daily ore trains from Belvoir Junction, to the steelworks at Rutherglen near Glasgow on Mondays and Thursdays, to Consett in Durham on Fridays, and to South Bank, Middlesbrough on Saturdays. On Tuesdays and Wednesdays two trains also ran to South Bank and Consett respectively.

Steam locomotives were used in the quarries, mainly 0–6–0 tanks, which were usually given local names. These often had

Figure 24.2   In 1950 Robert Stephenson and Hawthorns Ltd built the first seven 0–6–0ST locomotives of an eventual class of ten to meet the requirements of Stewarts and Lloyds Minerals Ltd. Similar to the famous **Austerity**, *they were, in fact, of a different design, the most apparent evidence of this being a shorter saddle tank. Nine of them were employed in the quarries and steelworks of the Corby area. One, the last to be built in 1958, was delivered new to Harlaxton Quarries. Named* **Achilles**, *and seen here at Harlaxton on 9 September 1961, it was destined to have a very short life, being scrapped in November 1969*
© D Swift

Figure 24.3   The 0–6–0 saddle tank Denton, *at Denton on 9 September 1961. Built by Andrew Barclay & Sons in 1951, she was one of those quarry engines given local names. A sister engine,* Salmon, *which also spent most of its working life in these quarries has been preserved and can be seen at the Rutland Railway Museum at Cottesmore*
© D Swift

The 200-foot rise of the escarpment was overcome by providing a reversal point halfway up. At its steepest, the incline was 1 in 20 with a ruling gradient of 1 in 40. The branch ended alongside the minor road between Croxton Kerrial and Grantham. The Stanton Ironworks Company, later Stewarts and Lloyds Minerals, built other lines from here to reach their various quarries, as well as another maintenance workshop.

From the early 1970s British Steel increasingly imported foreign ore of a higher grade than was found in Britain, and home production fell. On 15 February 1974 Denton Sidings were closed, and on 14 February 1974 the last iron ore train left Harlaxton and the branch closed the following day.

From 15 February 1976, however, for a short time, production started up again. The overgrown track to Casthorpe Junction was traversed by a test train consisting of two Class 20 diesel locomotives with two brake vans, and pronounced safe. A new

Figure 24.4 *Denton's busy sidings, with loaded wagons awaiting despatch, on 1 November 1973* © Author

Figure 24.5 *The quarry workshops at Denton in 1973. The truck is standing on the 'main' line to Harston; the track to the left once led to the quarries in Denton Park* © Author

problems hauling trains up the incline to Harlaxton. Diesels, introduced in 1967, were more powerful and overcame this.

The method of working was that wagons would be brought from Belvoir Junction to the exchange-sidings at Denton and Casthorpe Junction, from where they would be taken to the quarry faces by the mining company's locomotives. The latter were also to be seen, more regularly in later years, on British Railways' lines. Belvoir Junction to Denton was worked one engine in steam, and subject to a 20 mph speed limit. In 1960 six trains were required daily. Towards the end 20 000 tons a week were despatched from the Harlaxton quarries and 10 000 tons from Woolsthorpe.

face was opened but as all sidings had been removed the ore was taken by dumper truck to Casthorpe Junction, and from there to Etruria in Staffordshire or Shotton in North Wales.

At their greatest extent some 9½ miles of quarry railway were built in this area, with five miles of branch railway. There is some very attractive countryside, successfully restored after quarrying, but there is much still to be seen, both former railway

routes and the Grantham Canal, but it is difficult to imagine just how busy the area once was.

At least one of the steam engines used on the system still survives: an 0–6–0 saddle tank, *Salmon*, built by Andrew Barclay of Kilmarnock in 1942, was used for most of its life here. Withdrawn in 1968 it was purchased privately and it became the second locomotive of the North Yorkshire Moors Railway.

Figure 24.6 *The last load of ironstone to be taken out by train from Harlaxton Quarry on 22 February 1974. In the distance are the lines locomotive sheds, and the 'main' line leading eventually to Belvoir Junction. The rusting rails to the right ran into another quarry face* © *Grantham Journal*

Figure 24.7 *A British Steel Corporation 0–4–0 shunter waits as the last truckload of ironstone to be quarried at Harlaxton is loaded on the 22 February 1974, following which the system was closed. Part of the line had a brief renaissance two years later, but no trains were to run again in this quarry* © *Grantham Journal*

25

Ironstone Railways South of Grantham

The existence of iron-ore in workable quantities was first proved in the parishes of Sproxton, Buckminster, Sewstern and Colsterworth in 1885. Another seven years were to pass, however, before the first quarry would open. The reason for this delay was probably partly the lack of a nearby railway line for quarry lines to connect to, industrial railway routes tending to be relatively short.

South of Grantham, on the borders of Lincolnshire, Leicestershire and Rutland, there grew and operated, over three quarters of a century, an extensive network of lines devoted solely to the extraction and despatch of iron-ore. Two of these lines fall within the geographical area of this book, and a third, whilst outside the geographical area, linked with the Midland Railway route between Saxby and Little Bytham, included elsewhere in this book, and for this reason is pertinent to this chapter.

These lines are

1. Highdyke to Sproxton and Stainby which served the Colsterworth and Sproxton Quarries;
2. Buckminster Sidings to Stainby, for the quarries around Stainby and Sewstern; and
3. Pain's Sidings to Market Overton providing an outlet for the quarries around the latter village.

The lines serving the former two areas were linked although their ore was despatched to two separate steelworks, Colsterworth ore to Frodingham via Grantham, and Stainby ore to Melton Mowbray via Saxby. Market Overton ore was also sent to Melton Mowbray. In later years ore from the two latter areas went to Corby via Saxby.

The opening of the Saxby to Bourne link by the Midland Railway in 1891 gave rail access to the iron-ore field, and in 1892 the Holwell Iron Company began working ore adjacent to

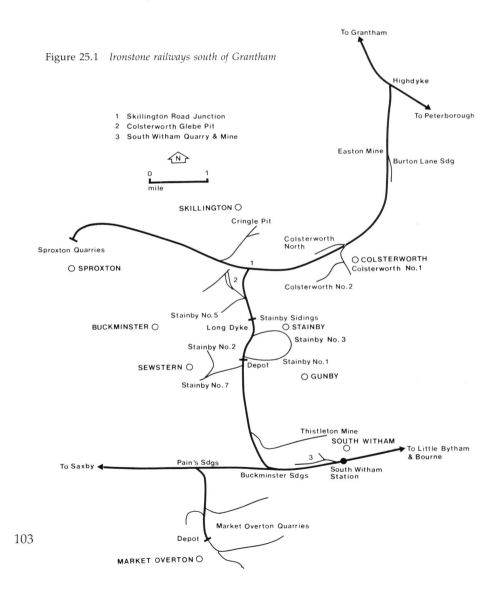

Figure 25.1 *Ironstone railways south of Grantham*

the line, by the site of what was to become Buckminster Sidings. In 1898, Stainby Number 1 Pit was opened and a line, 2¼ miles long, was built by the company from Buckminster Sidings to the pit. A locomotive depot and workshops were established south of the level-crossing with the road between Gunby and Sewstern.

In 1906 James Pain Ltd began quarrying at Market Overton, initially to the north of the village, near to the point where they established their own railway workshop. They also built their own branch from the Midland Railway at Pain's Sidings to their workings. This was shortly after extended to their pits to the

Figure 25.2 *Colsterworth No 1 Quarry in its early days. Of particular interest are the two excavators, both steam driven. That in the foreground is removing the overburden to expose the ironstone bed on which it stands. The overburden was carried on the gantry to the rear of the quarry, to be used later for restoration purposes as the working face moved forwards. Further down the quarry the ironstone is being removed by the second excavator, which would load direct into trucks*   © G R Rowe

south and east of the village. In 1908 the Holwell Ironstone Company opened a Number 2 Pit at Stainby.

To the east of South Witham Station in 1895, the Holwell Ironstone Company had also started a small limestone quarry. In 1907 they established a replacement quarry adjacent to the station, building a narrow-gauge tramway of 2' 8½" within it on which horses pulled skips of stone to a hoist, the quarry floor being thirty feet below main-railway-line level. The hoist lifted the skips to discharge them into standard-gauge railway wagons. In 1930 the narrow-gauge track had become so extensive that internal-combustion-engined locomotives were introduced. It was to be from this limestone quarry that the Stanton Ironworks Company were, in 1944, to establish an underground iron-ore mine, adits being driven underground from the quarry face.

The demand for munitions following the outbreak of the First World War led to calls for the increased production of iron and steel. To meet this development of fresh iron-ore fields was encouraged. The Frodingham Iron and Steel Company leased land at Colsterworth, but had no rail outlet, and in 1915 the construction of a line southwards from Highdyke on the East Coast Main Line, half-a-mile north of Stoke Tunnel was proposed. This line which included a stiff gradient climbing away from Highdyke, where there were a number of exchange-sidings, was to be built through Colsterworth to Stainby by the Great Northern Railway (GNR). The Holwell Ironstone Company were prompted to extend their line a futher half mile to Stainby, and start working their Number 3 Pit. The GNR opened their branch as far as Colsterworth Number 1 Pit in 1918, where the Frodingham Iron and Steel Company also built their locomotive depot. Shortly afterwards, the line was extended to Stainby where a number of exchange-sidings were built. The limit of the GNR Branch was at Long Dyke, a point a few yards south of Stainby Sidings, where an end-on junction was made with the quarry railway system.

The construction of these new railways meant that the following years were ones of expansion, and in 1924 Stainby

Figure 25.3   *The junction of the quarry lines and British Rail was at Long Dyke, immediately south of Stainby Sidings. The signal giving access to the southern end of these sidings can be seen through the bridge in this view taken in April 1974*
© Author

Number 7 Pit was started. The Parkgate Iron and Steel Company leased land at Sproxton, and in 1925 the three-mile line from Skillington Road Junction to Sproxton was opened. This was destined to be the very last new line mooted by the GNR before it disappeared in the grouping of 1923, and became part of the London and North Eastern Railway (LNER). In 1926, both Colsterworth Number 2 and Colsterworth Glebe Pits were opened, and in the early 1930s, Cringle Pit.

By the mid-1930s, both James Pain Ltd and the Holwell Ironstone Company had become part of the Stanton Ironworks Company, who operated and maintained over ten miles of track in the area.

The output from the Highdyke branches was such that in 1931 there were thirteen trains each way daily provided by the LNER. In 1935 this had fallen to eleven. They were assembled at Highdyke into three daily trains to Frodingham, two to Colwick, and one to Parkgate, all via Grantham. By 1938 the number of daily branch trains had risen to fifteen. The Second World War again created enormous demands for home-produced iron and steel, and increased output required more trains. As a result, from Highdyke there were four trains to Frodingham, and one each to Colwick, Parkgate, Scotland and Teeside. There were also two Sunday trains to Frodingham, and another, if required, to Teeside.

In 1944 an underground mine was opened at South Witham, from the bed of the limestone quarry. This mine continued in operation until 1955 when, now in the ownership of Stewarts and Lloyds, it was closed, to be replaced by the same company's Thistleton Mine, half a mile to the north, the same year. This new mine was served by a new length of railway line, one mile long, and in its galleries ran twelve-ton mine cars, hauled by diesel, and overhead-wire electric locomotives on a 3' 6" gauge system.

A third mine at Easton, north of Colsterworth, was opened by the United Steel Company in 1958, adjacent to Burton Lane Siding.

The following year on 3 March 1959, British Railways closed

and South Witham closed also. From 11 April the line was again cut back, this time to Pain's Siding from Buckminster Siding.

From now on the history gets somewhat complicated. Market Overton quarries were still operating, their ore being removed via Saxby. In March 1966 the Saxby to Pain's Siding line was closed, and Pain's Siding to Buckminster Siding reopened to be worked by Stewarts and Lloyds, removing the ore via Highdyke. However, in September the same year, this stretch again closed. Also in 1966, the United Steel Company closed Easton Mine.

On 2 October 1967, the Pain's Siding to Buckminster Siding line reopened yet again, this time remaining in use until the final closure of the Market Overton Quarry in January 1972. From 19 October 1972 the line south of Skillington Road Junction closed and from 6 August 1973 the final length, Highdyke to Sproxton followed, bringing to an end eighty years of quarrying in the area.

There remained at Market Overton a modern two-road engine

Figure 25.4　*Pains's Sidings in 1974. The track in the foreground is the former Midland Railway line between Saxby and Little Bytham, the Market Overton branch going off to the right*　　　© Tim Mawson

the former Midland Railway and Great Northern Joint Railway and its former Midland Railway western extension from Little Bytham through to Saxby. Much closed completely but some sections were retained for goods traffic. One of these was from Saxby to South Witham, for the ironstone traffic.

The 1960s were dramatic days for the quarries, mines and their railway connections. The United Kingdom was becoming less dependent on home-quarried ironstone, with increasing foreign imports of a higher ore content, and retraction of the industry began in earnest.

In 1964 Thistleton Mine and South Witham Quarry were closed, and from 6 April the line between Buckminster Siding

Figure 25.5.　*A view near the eastern end of the Sproxton Branch in October 1974*
© Author

Figure 25.6 *Former NCB 0–6–0 saddle tank,* Primrose No 2, *being moved by the yard shunter, a former BR Class 03 0–6–0 204 bhp diesel, D2381, at Market Overton on 29 November 1973. D2381 can now be seen performing similar duties at Steamtown, Carnforth.* Primrose No 2, *a Hunslet built in 1951, (Works Number 3715), is now at the Yorkshire Dales Railway*
© Author

shed and workshop, with other workshops at Stainby – an attractive proposition for anyone involved in the business of railway preservation. This, together with the junction onto the

Figure 25.7 *On 7 November 1973, the famous Gresley Pacific, No 4472* Flying Scotsman, *attacks the bank from Highdyke Junction, heading for Market Overton*
© Grantham Journal

East Coast Main Line attracted Flying Scotsman Enterprises, and Market Overton, in railway terms, had its finest hour. It became the home of two very famous engines, *Flying Scotsman* and *Pendennis Castle*, together with a large number of industrial steam-locomotives and a variety of rolling stock. *Flying Scotsman* first came on 20 October 1973, and both main-line engines could occasionally be seen wending their way slowly through the now tranquil landscape to work special trains on the national network.

Another distinguished visitor was the Southern Railway 'Merchant Navy' class, 4–6–2, No 35029, *Ellerman Lines*. Rescued from Barry scrapyard in 1973 by the National Railway Museum, it was taken to the Stainby workshops, there to be sectioned to enable museum visitors to view the inner workings of a steam-locomotive. It now rests in the Railway Museum in York.

A proposal to establish a privately owned public steam-railway on the line unfortunately came to nothing, and almost a year after they had first arrived, the main-line engines and much of the stock left and on 16 September 1974 the Highdyke Junction was severed. Shortly after, in 1975, the track was lifted, leaving only the nucleus of a small museum devoted to the ironstone railways at Market Overton, known as the Market Overton Industrial Railway Association. In 1979 this moved to a new site at Cottesmore and became what is now the Rutland Railway Museum.

In 1980 the reinstatement of the Highdyke/Sproxton Line was mooted to serve one of three coalmines to be established in the Vale of Belvoir, but this was ruled out, partly because of British Rail's being unwilling to recreate a junction on the then recently upgraded East Coast Main Line at this point.

Figure 25.8   *Southern Railway 'Merchant Navy' Class 4–6–2, No 35029* Ellerman Lines *was rescued in 1973 from the Barry scrapyard. It can be seen today in the National Railway Museum in York. Eleven tons of metal were removed from one side of the locomotive to enable visitors to see the internal workings of a steam-engine. The work was carried out at the former quarry depot at Stainby in 1974, and had just been completed when this photograph was taken*   © Tim Mawson

Sleaford to Bourne

If they had still been around on 22 September 1930, the Directors of the Great Northern Railway would have heaved a sigh of relief. On this day the line they did not want to build lost its passenger service. They received the Act to build it in 1865 but sought power to abandon it in 1868. This was, however, refused by the Board of Trade who required completion by June 1871. In fact the single-line route opened for goods in October 1871, and passenger trains started running on 2 January 1872. The line was sixteen miles long, with stations at Aswarby and Scredington, Billingborough and Horbling, Rippingdale, and Morton Road; of these only Billingborough and Horbling boasted two platforms. A service of five passenger trains each way daily sufficed for its traffic, with one extra on Mondays. The journey time was fifty minutes, making the average speed about twenty miles an hour.

Figure 26.2   Morton Road Station in February 1961, with a very respectable number of wagons in the yard   © D Thompson

Figure 26.1   Sleaford to Bourne

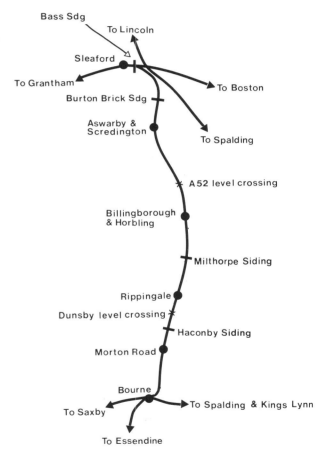

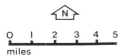

ESSENDINE, BOURNE, AND SLEAFORD BRANCH

(SINGLE LINE—STAFF STATIONS, ESSENDINE, BOURNE, BILLINGBORO' AND SLEAFORD.)

DOWN.

Stations: ESSENDINE ... dep. / Braceboro' Spa. / Wilsthorpe Siding / Thurlby / BOURNE arr. dep. / Morton road / Haconby siding / Rippingale / Milthorpe sidin' / BILLINGBRO' arr. dep. / Aswarby / Burton siding / SLEAFORD arr.

Distance from Essendine: 2¾ / 3 / 4 / 4½ / 4½ / 6 / 9 / 10 / 12 / 13 / 15 / 16¾ / 20 / 21 / 24 / 24½

Notes:
- F Wagons for Haconby Siding to be taken to Billingboro' and returned next day on 28 up.
- G Stops at Milthorpe Siding when necessary to attach perishable traffic.
- The combined loads of these three trains must not exceed 80 wagons.
- Load limited to 25 wagons.
- Commences 25th May, 1928.
- After working 22 up to work 25 up.
- From Westwood train 41, page 5.

UP.

Stations: SLEAFORD ... dep. / Burton siding / Aswarby / BILLINGBRO' arr. dep. / Milthorpe siding / Rippingale / Haconby siding / Morton road / BOURNE arr. dep. / Thurlby / Wilsthorpe Siding / Braceboro' Spa. / ESSENDINE Stn. arr.

Distance from Sleaford: 2¾ / 3¼ / 8 / 9 / 10 / 11¾ / 13½ / 14½ / 17¾ / 19¾ / 21½ / 24½

Notes:
- On Mondays leaves Billingboro' at 8.59 a.m. and runs 2 minutes later to Bourne.
- 4 minutes recovery time allowed at Morton Road.
- Train must be despatched from Morton Road at 2.18 p.m. if practicable.
- E May convey Wagons of Cattle from Sleaford market.
- When running late and not conveying goods wagons mixed trains must run at passenger train speed between stations.
- To Peterboro' Spiral train 881, p. 33.
- Commences 25th May, train 20, p. 157.

At Billingborough the opening had been looked forward to and the villagers planned to celebrate the event. Unfortunately, they were not told of the date until three days before and by then it was too late to do all they wanted to. But the church bells were rung, and people thronged the station to view the trains which were decorated with flags and evergreens.

Complaints were immediately made about timing because although the first train from Sleaford was due in Bourne at 7.5 am there was no Essendine connection until 8.5 am, or to Spalding until 10.20 am, so that onward travellers were faced with a wait of one hour or of two and a quarter hours. This was of no use to businessmen, particularly those wanting to travel regularly to London, via Essendine.

Billingborough was once the host of an annual Horse Fair, held in June, and the station here was the destination, and point of departure, of hundreds of horses and many visitors until just after the First World War.

There were goods sidings at each of the stations. In addition, public delivery sidings were provided at Milthorpe and Haconby. A small brickworks, Burton Brickworks, was established alongside the line, one mile north of Aswarby and Scredington Station, with rail connection. Finally, from 1899 to 1905 the Bass Maltings were built at Sleaford. These still exist, and there is little in English industrial architecture that can match the scale of the building – a row of eight detached six-storey blocks with a massive square tower at the centre. They were also provided with sidings from the line.

The introduction of the Winter Timetable in September 1930 was a milestone in the closure of railways in Britain. On that

Figure 26.4 *The branch goods train, with a Gresley J6 0–6–0 locomotive at Billingborough Station before the section of the line north of here to Sleaford closed in 1956*   Courtesy Grimsby Public Library

day ninety-nine stations and seventeen lines were closed including the one from Sleaford to Bourne. (This record number of station closures was not exceeded until 15 June 1964 at the height of the Beeching era, when 106 stations closed.) The reason for the closures was a well-known one – increasing competition from road transport. After September 1930 the only passenger trains on the branch were occasional Sunday Stamford and Bourne to Skegness excursions which called at all stations, but these ceased in 1939. However, one daily goods train continued to run, from Sleaford to Bourne and return.

The last through passenger train to use the branch was hauled

Figure 26.3 (On facing page) *Working timetable, September 1927. The daily goods train, 28 Up, left Grantham at 9.7 am, calling at Honington and Ancaster, and Rauceby when required, reaching Sleaford at 10.39 am. The return journey, 60 Down, spent 3¼ hours at Sleaford, before continuing to Grantham at 12.35 am, making the same calls as in the morning. Grantham was reached at 1.43 am. Note that Up trains stopped at Burton Sidings and at Haconby and Milthorpe Sidings when required. Down trains could stop at Milthorpe if required, but the other two were served by Up trains only*   Courtesy E Neve

dant mineral wagons. A five-and-a-half-mile ribbon of these, broken only by level-crossings, could be seen south from Sleaford to the A52 at Threekingham for some years. The remainder of the branch, to Billingborough, retained its good services until 2 April 1965, when this, along with the, by then, goods-only

Figure 26.6　*Billingborough North signal box and level-crossing in 1961. Although the line north of here was used for storing redundant wagons, access was gained from the Sleaford end. When this photograph was taken, this part of the line had not been used for five years. In 1962 the gates and the rails north of this station were removed*
© *Richard Goodman*

Figure 26.5　*Aswarby and Scredington Station in 1972. The station and goods shed were an example of the sort of provision for freight and passengers which the amount of subsequent traffic could never justify*
© *Author*

by a Boston K2 2–6–0, No 61743, and the occasion was a Railway Correspondence and Travel Society special tour, 'The Fensman', which took place on 9 September 1956, a few weeks after closure to goods traffic of the section from Sleaford to Billingborough on July 28th. On this date Aswarby and Scredington Station closed also. The track remained to Billingborough for some years afterwards and was used for the storage of redun-

branch from Spalding to Bourne also closed, although no train had run between Haconby Siding and Billingborough since 15 June 1964. Traffic towards the end was mainly potatoes and grain. In the season, trains of twenty-five to thirty wagons of potatoes would come off the branch.

Services on the line were never frequent – on one occasion between the wars it is said that the Dunsby level-crossing gate-keeper and his family used a platelayer's pump trolley to take them and their luggage to Bourne to catch the train for their holiday!

The stations are still intact and in a reasonable state of repair. Indeed, at Rippingale, after twenty years of closure, the enamel station signboard can still be seen on the wall of the building. This station, although now a modern house, has been tastefully renovated to retain all its period charm, and is probably the best example of a now disused railway station in the county.

Figure 26.7   Shunting taking place at Rippingale in February 1961. In common with other stations on the branch, the main building displays some very attractive roof-design details, quite common on early railway buildings   © D Thompson

27

The Midland and Great Northern Railway Western Section Kings Lynn to Saxby and Peterborough

The Midland and Great Northern Railway was one of the two most famous Joint Lines in the country, the other being the Somerset and Dorset. It ran from Little Bytham and Peterborough in the west, to Cromer, Norwich and Yarmouth in the east and retained a separate identity from 1893, until it was absorbed by the London and North Eastern Railway in 1936. It was almost 200 miles in length, with a great variety of trains working an intensive service, complicated by much of it being single track. This chapter is concerned only with what was known as the Western Section, that is, from Kings Lynn in the east to Peterborough and Saxby, via Little Bytham, in the west. At Little Bytham it made an end-on junction with the Midland Railway and it was their metals that ran westwards from this point. It is the Saxby to Kings Lynn Line that this chapter concerns.

The Western Section was built in seven stages, and five different companies were involved. This is characteristic of the building of the complete system.

The Norwich and Spalding Railway Company (NSR) were first on the scene. They opened the first part of their proposed Spalding–Wisbech line between the Great Northern Railway station at Spalding, opened in 1848, and Holbeach on 3 May 1858. It was single-line and eight miles long, with four of its own stations. Two, Weston and Whaplode, had no sidings. On 1 July 1862 the NSR extended it nine miles to Sutton Bridge, again single-line, and with another four stations. Two years later the Lynn and Sutton Bridge, added thirteen double-track miles, with yet again four stations, the western most one being South Lynn, near to Kings Lynn, which eventually became the point at which the Western Section of the Midland and Great

Figure 27.1   *Holbeach Station around the turn of the century. Three railway staff and a postman pose on the platform as a goods train passes. In the distance Holbeach West box can be seen. One of two boxes controlling movements in the area, it guarded the western end of the station loop, and entry to the goods yard*   © D Waters

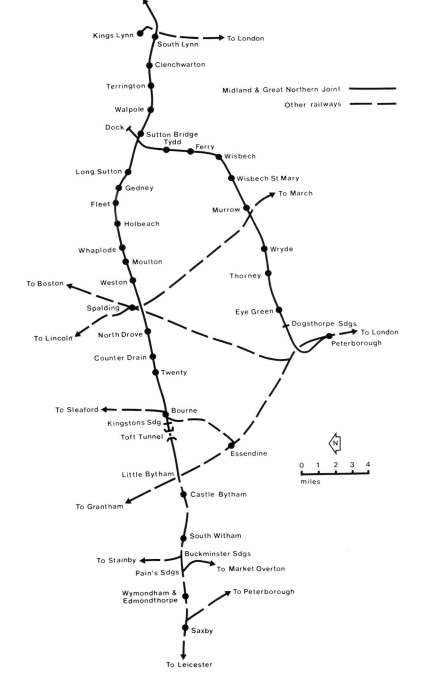

To Yarmouth

Kings Lynn
South Lynn — To London

Clenchwarton

Terrington

Walpole

Dock

Sutton Bridge
Tydd
Ferry
Wisbech

Wisbech St Mary

To March

Long Sutton
Gedney
Fleet
Murrow

Holbeach

Wryde

Whaplode
Moulton
Thorney

To Boston
Weston

Spalding
Eye Green
Dogsthorpe Sdgs
To London

To Lincoln
North Drove
Peterborough

Counter Drain

Twenty

To Sleaford
Bourne

Kingstons Sdg
Toft Tunnel

Essendine

Little Bytham

Castle Bytham

To Grantham

South Witham

To Stainby
Buckminster Sdgs
Pain's Sdgs
To Market Overton

Wymondham &
Edmondthorpe
To Peterborough

Saxby

To Leicester

Midland & Great Northern Joint ——————
Other railways – – – – –

N

0 1 2 3 4
miles

Figure 27.2 *The Midland and Great Northern Railway Western Section, Kings Lynn to Little Bytham and Peterborough*

Northern Railway met the Eastern Section. This opened on 1 November 1864.

In its route across the fenland, the line had to cross the rivers which drained into the Wash, and these were substantial obstacles. Leaving Sutton Bridge the Rivers Nene and Ouse had to be overcome. At Sutton Bridge there was an existing swing-bridge, 314 feet long, taking the road over the Nene, a busy shipping route to Wisbech. This was simply converted to a road/rail bridge by running a single line along the road. However, the weight of the engines and trains put too much strain on the structure, and a new bridge became necessary.

Figure 27.3 *Cross Keys Bridge, at Sutton Bridge, in 1918. It had been opened in 1897, replacing an earlier bridge a hundred yards downstream. The engine is one of thirty-three 4–4–0 inside-cylinder passenger engines, built by Sharp, Stewart and Co, delivered to the M&GN from 1893 onwards. Attached to the rear of the train are two horseboxes*
© Ralph Bates

Figure 27.4 *Because the present Cross Keys Bridge was built upstream of its predecessor, realignment of the approach required some rebuilding of Sutton Bridge Station. As a result, it had an unusual 'S' shape, illustrated here in 1961. The main platform was an island, with a bay at the western end, used by Spalding and Peterborough trains which terminated here. Its position is indicated by the gap in the platform awning* © Richard Goodman

And so the now well known Cross Keys swing-bridge, with separate road and rail routes, was built, opening in 1897. At the same time, because of the reorganisation of the line to cross it, a new Sutton Bridge Station was built. Cross Keys still exists, although now carrying two roadways, and is a familiar landmark for travellers on this busy road between Norfolk and the Midlands.

The crossing of the River Ouse half a mile west of South Lynn Station produced the West Lynn Bridge, a girder bridge 490 feet long. The tidal rise and fall here enabled ships to pass underneath and so a fixed span could be used. It was the poor state of this bridge, together with what was claimed to be an exorbitant estimate for the cost of its repair, that was eventually used as one of the main arguments for closure of the railway.

Two more, separate, sections of the overall route opened on 1 August 1866. Spalding to Bourne, and Peterborough to Sutton Bridge, via Wisbech.

The Great Northern Railway (GNR) built between Spalding and Bourne. Like most of the lines east of Bourne, this new one crossed the flat, fertile fenland, to the GNR's Bourne Station, which had opened with the Essendine Branch in 1860. This too was single-line, (later doubled between Bourne and Twenty), nine miles long, and had three intermediate stations, Twenty, Counter Drain and North Drove.

Bourne was a unique station, having a small Tudor manor house as a booking office and the Stationmaster's home. It had once been owned by Sir Everard Digby, who was involved in the Gunpowder Plot with the notorious Guy Fawkes.

The three intermediate stations served no villages, simply scattered farmhouses, and it was difficult to decide on names for them. There are two theories as how Twenty got its name; one is that it was built in a field with that number on the Ordnance Survey map of the time, and the other that it was near a roadside milestone reading 20 miles to Colsterworth on the Great North Road. As the distance between Twenty and Colsterworth is only 15½ miles the former explanation seems more likely! Whatever the origin of the name 'Twenty', it undoubtedly gave rise to a well known railway riddle, which asks 'How many stations between Bourne and Spalding?' to which the answer was, 'Two and Twenty'! Counter Drain and North Drove both took their names from the drainage dykes on the banks of which they were built.

The line opened by the Peterborough, Wisbech and Sutton Bridge Railway was twenty-six miles long, with eight intermediate stations including Wisbech. Eight months later the section for both goods and passengers from 1 May 1894. Bourne to Little Bytham was six miles of double-track with no stations; the next thirteen miles ran single-line through to Saxby with three intermediate stations. One mile west of Bourne West Junction with the GNR's Essendine Branch, was the only tunnel on the joint system, Toft Tunnel, of some 330 yards, together with the steepest gradient, 1 in 100, west of the tunnel.

At a point three quarters of a mile east of Toft Tunnel a siding was provided to serve a brickworks, Kingston's Siding.

Another short section also opened on 15 May 1893. This was the Spalding–Avoiding Line, one and a quarter miles of double-track, built south of the town, to enable through-trains to avoid a reversal here.

The companies which made up the through-route from Yarmouth to Little Bytham, with their various branches, were

Figure 27.5 *An eastbound local of three coaches and a grimy Class 4MT 2–6–0 locomotive, leaves Bourne in 1958. Bourne Station was built in the garden of Red Hall, a Tudor manor house, the building behind the engine. For many years it was the Stationmaster's house. The Bourne engine shed can be seen between the platform buildings and the footbridge steps* Courtesy Grimsby Public Library

GNR opened their Spalding–March Line, eventually to become part of the Great Northern and Great Eastern Joint Railway. The two lines crossed, on the level, at Murrow, where there were stations on both lines.

Wisbech was a port on the River Nene, and riverside quays were served by a harbour branch, from the Wisbech goods yard, in use by 1872.

The Midland Railway were next on the scene, with their line from Bourne to Saxby, opened in two stages, Bourne to Little Bytham for goods only from 15 May 1893 and the complete

Figure 27.6 *Twenty Station, looking west. Removal of the signal arm indicates that this view was taken after the passenger service had been withdrawn. The chequered post on the left holds the tablet-catching apparatus. Originally single-track, the Bourne–Twenty stretch was doubled in 1894; the second platform then needed here, that on the left, had to be sited in a rather curious 'half-staggered' position relative to the one on the right, the signal box precluding its construction exactly opposite* © M Black

Figure 27.7 *The western portal of Toft Tunnel, 330 yards long, in April, 1974*
© Author

formed into the Midland and Great Northern Joint Railway on 1 July 1893. At Little Bytham it made an end-on junction with the Midland, where there was no station, only an isolated signal box controlling the point where the double-track became single.

In addition to local passenger services calling at intermediate stations, the line also carried long distance through-trains. Prior to the opening west of Bourne, trains from Kings Lynn ran through to Essendine. Eventually, there were Cromer–Peterborough, Peterborough–Norwich, and even Cromer–Kings Cross via Peterborough trains daily. The most well known train, the one which ran right to the end, was the Yarmouth–Leicester, or the 'Leicester' as it was known. In the 1930s three separate

trains left Lowestoft, Norwich and Cromer, combined at Melton Constable, reached Leicester and formed the stock for the run through Birmingham to Gloucester. At the weekends, express trains, some with restaurant cars attached, ran to Yarmouth from Manchester, Nottingham, Derby, Halifax and Birmingham.

The timings of the express and local trains were further complicated by the schedules for goods trains, and it was for the variety and number of its goods trains that the Joint is often best remembered. In fact, this traffic was usually of far greater importance than were passengers from the intermediate stations.

The Fens, being exceptionally fertile, produce abundant crops and were a valuable source of revenue. Soon after Christmas flowers were important, and special steam-heated vans carried thousands of tons of daffodils, narcissi, hyacinths and tulips. In the early Spring cabbage, broccoli and lettuces were sent to Covent Garden. From June to August soft fruit was in season, gooseberries, red and black currants, raspberries and strawberries, all needing careful handling, and, being perishable, regular, fast trains to convey them all over the country and to Ireland. Terrington, Walpole, Sutton Bridge, Wisbech, Wisbech St Mary, Murrow, Long Sutton, Gedney and Holbeach had daily trains to themselves, often loading as many as sixty wagons! As the year went on, peas, plums and apples were important, and in the winter potatoes and sugar beet.

To get this produce to the stations at Fleet and Wryde, narrow-gauge railways were built, the most extensive of which was at Fleet, where a system, built and operated by a local farming company, ran for some fifteen miles northwards into Holbeach Marsh. Opened in stages from 1918, it reached its maximum mileage, including a number of branches, in the early 1930s. It was at first horse-worked; the horses were replaced in 1923 by two petrol-engined locomotives which were themselves replaced by a diminutive diesel engine in 1925, and it eventually ceased operation in 1955. At Wryde there were two lines, one north and one south from the station yard. The date of their construction is not known. The smaller of the two ran from the east end of the goods yard south for about half a mile, to a point adjacent to what is now the A47 main road. It is believed to have closed about the time of the Second World War. The other, to the north of the Joint Line, also ran from the goods yard, westwards parallel to the main line and across the road adjacent to the station level-crossing. It then turned north, and east, to run into the fenland fields for one and a half miles. It is believed to have been last used in the early 1950s. It is likely that because of their short length, the wagons were hauled by horses.

Agricultural traffic accounted for about ninety per cent of the goods traffic originating on the Western Section, but there were other important factors. In the Peterborough area were the extensive brick fields of the London Brick Company. Two of these works, at Dogsthorpe and at Eye Green, were connected to the Midland and Great Northern Railway, and called for daily trains. The import of timber from Scandinavia to the ports at Sutton Bridge and Wisbech also required special trains.

Sutton Bridge was the location for a disastrous foray into the development of a port by the Sutton Bridge Dock Company. In 1881 they completed a thirteen-acre dock to the west of the River Nene, with a short length of railway running for almost half a mile down to it. The first vessel entered it on 8 June. The next day the ground adjacent to the entrance lock subsided. Despite trainloads of fill being brought in, 500 feet of facing from the western side collapsed into the dock one month later. With difficulty, three boats inside were safely removed and it was never used again. Its remains can still be seen, now as part of a golf course. The riverside wharf continued in use, however, together with the branch railway.

At the western end of the line, from the Midland Railway west of Little Bytham, branches northwards from Buckminster Sidings to Stainby in 1898, and south from Pain's Sidings to Market Overton in 1906, were built to ironstone quarries. Part of the main line here remained open until 1972 for this traffic, which is dealt with in more detail in Chapter 25.

Figure 27.8 *The junction at Buckminster Sidings on 1 November 1973. The single-track line here, west of Little Bytham, was part of the Midland Railway. The site of the sidings is to the right of the main line, and the privately owned ironstone branch goes off to the right. At the time its only use was to give access to the Market Overton workshops, from Highdyke Junction, with the East Coast Main Line. The workshops were used by Flying Scotsman Enterprises and were the home of a number of preserved steam-locomotives, carriages and trucks*   © Author

Because of increasing maintenance costs, including the need to replace West Lynn Bridge, and because of falling revenue, closure of the whole line to passenger traffic, and complete closure of several sections, were mooted in 1958. Prior to this there had been, for such an extensive system, remarkably few station closures. On 2 December 1957 Wryde, Thorney and Eye Green closed for passengers. On 15 September 1958 the last passenger alighted at North Drove. One line closure had come after subsidence of part of the Spalding–Avoiding Line in 1955, and it fell out of use soon after.

Protest gave no reward, and the Midland and Great Northern Joint Railway closed on 2 March 1959, the last trains running on 28 February, amid scenes of great sadness and celebration. At Bourne, the last passenger train arrived at 9.20 pm from Spalding carrying the Royal Train Headcode. The last westbound train called at 9.4 pm on its way from Saxby to Spalding. Normally only four tickets were sold at Bourne for this, but on this night there were ninety-four travellers. Many of these changed at Twenty and thus managed to travel on both trains. At Murrow, the last Peterborough–Melton Constable train was seen off by 250 villagers and the local band, who together

Figure 27.9   The attractive station at Eye Green in September 1968, shortly after recovery of the track. The lattice fencing is typical of Joint Line stations   © Author

Figure 27.10   The engine crew of the last passenger train to leave Holbeach Station, the 5.57 pm from Spalding on 28 February 1959   © D Waters

delayed it for twenty minutes. At Wisbech, the same train passed to a firework display.

Not all was lost, however, for several lengths remained open for goods.

One of these was Spalding to Bourne, from where another goods branch still ran northwards to Billingborough on the former Sleaford Line. The farm traffic was the reason for its retention, mainly potatoes and sugar beet. Trains were run as required, usually one every two-to-three days, but every day during the beet season. Twenty, Counter Drain and North Drove closed from 30 March 1964, and Bourne and the Billingborough Branch on 5 April 1965.

Another was the line running eastwards from Spalding to Sutton Bridge. Fenland farm-produce traffic was still very heavy at this time, mainly for flowers, fruit and potatoes, canned goods from Lockwoods factory at Long Sutton, as well as occasional timber trains. Even though they had no sidings, Weston and Whaplode loaded crated vegetables and parcels from their platforms. These two stations, together with Fleet and Gedney, closed on 3 February 1964, Moulton closed on 15 June 1964, and ten months later the remaining goods yards and the line, closed completely, together with the Bourne Line. To the end, a daily train was required with fourteen-to-fifteen wagons, but with up to forty wagons in the seed potato season.

At Murrow, the Midland and Great Northern Railway crossed on the level the Great Northern and Great Eastern Joint Railway. Closure of the line involved the demolition of the overbridge north of Peterborough which carried trains eventually into the station. But agricultural traffic and bricks still called for retention of the line from Wisbech to Dogsthorpe. To reach this, a south to west curve was built at Murrow, and trains to and in between these two points worked, via this, from March. On 13 July 1964 Wryde Station was closed, and on 28 December 1964, Thorney, Wisbech St Mary and Wisbech were closed, together with the Murrow–Wisbech Line. Brick trains were the last users, and ran from Dogsthorpe until the final closure of this last vestige of the Midland and Great Northern Railway, Western Section, on 18 April 1966.

Figure 27.11 *A short brick train, with a Thompson Class B1 4–6–0 at its head, leaves Dogsthorpe Sidings and heads in the direction of Murrow. The state of the track and the fact that the engine is working backwards to Murrow indicate that the photograph was taken after the rationalisation of the line in 1959* © E L Back

28

Edenham to Little Bytham

Nineteenth century landowners were notorious for wanting the benefit of railway lines to the communities for which they were responsible, but also for ensuring that their parkland did not suffer from the intrusion of the new form of transport. With it they foresaw a loss of privacy and a demand for development. As a result, many lines were built on circuitious routes or in tunnels. A few, very few, took the opportunity to build their own private lines to serve their estate. One of these, unique in Lincolnshire was built by the 21st Lord Willoughby, of Grimsthorpe Castle, near Bourne. Lord Willoughby was an innovator, and in 1850 carried out his own trials using portable steam-engines for ploughing and driving machinery in the Estate farmyards. He was advised in the design of these engines by his friend, Daniel Gooch, the Locomotive Superintendent of the Great Western Railway.

The Great Northern Railway's (GNR) 'Towns' Line from Peterborough to Retford was opened in 1852, and Lord Willoughby took the decision to build a road from the nearest station, Little Bytham, around the edge of his deer park, to Edenham, just over one mile away from his family seat. To haul traffic along this road he bought a steam road-engine, which, in the event, proved unequal to the task of hauling economic loads on the steeper gradients.

To overcome this he decided, again with the advice of Gooch, to convert his road into a railway line, and this was done in 1855. Alterations to the alignment were made in places, to ease curves and gradients. The road-engine was converted into a railway-engine, two other small locomotives were purchased and the line opened for goods traffic. It was four miles long, with a small terminus at Edenham, three miles to the east of Bourne and a mile west of Grimsthorpe Castle. At Little Bytham the rails crossed a public road to enter the station yard,

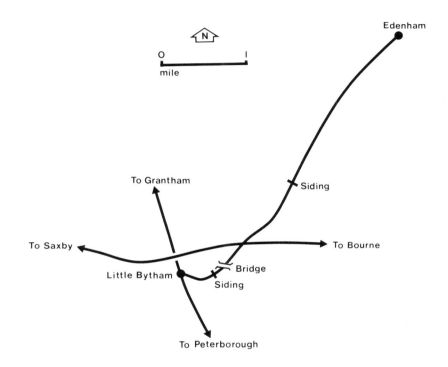

Figure 28.1 *Edenham to Little Bytham*

connecting with the GNR sidings. Apart from this, the line was constructed on land in the ownership of the Estate. There were also two intermediate sidings.

A public house, The Steam Plough (now called The Willoughby Arms), was built over the road from Little Bytham Station, and this in addition to providing for its normal function, was to serve as the booking office and waiting room for the

122

and fixed signals were needed on the approaches to both ends of the branch. It was in July 1857 that approval was finally given, by which time the track had been relaid with more sleepers and heavier rails. The line was subject to only one engine being in steam at any one time and to an overall speed limit of 15 mph with a reduction to 8 mph on curves. Mixed trains of passenger coaches and goods wagons began from 8 December 1857, providing a service of five trains each way a day. There was no Sunday service.

It was at this time that a new driver was needed for the line. William Stroudley, then working for the GNR as a foreman fitter at Peterborough was appointed, probably because he would also be able to maintain the locomotives. He stayed for less than a year, but went on eventually to become the Locomotive Superintendent of the London, Brighton and South Coast Railway from 1870 to 1889.

Figure 28.2 *The delightfully restored weighbridge cabin at the Edenham terminus. It illustrates the Victorian attention to the design of even the most humble buildings with its decorated ridge tiles and attractive chimney* © Author

Figure 28.3 *The bridge parapets on the road between Little Bytham and Witham on the Hill. This was one of two bridges on the branch, the other being over the River Glen a few yards away from Little Bytham Station* © Author

southern terminus. However, before a passenger service could be laid on an inspection by the Board of Trade was necessary.

The first inspection, in June 1856, found many defects: sleepers, points, rail joints and drainage were found to be defective; there were no gates to protect the Little Bytham level-crossing;

123

For a few years the line prospered. Edenham was the railhead for a wide area, including Bourne, and the yard was busy with passengers, coal and farm produce. However, in 1860 Bourne achieved its own connection with the main line, from Essendine, 3½ miles south of Little Bytham. Much of the traffic was immediately diverted to the new railway, and the heyday of the branch was over; it was left to serve only the needs of the Estate and it never recovered.

A public notice appeared in September 1866 stating that from the following month passenger coaches would be withdrawn. However, they were reinstated shortly after, and a token service was provided until 1871. Little money was available for maintenance and the engines and track deteriorated. Eary in 1872, following the disposal of the last of the engines, the line became horse-worked, closing for good in the summer of 1873. The track remained *in situ* until February 1890, when it and the remaining trucks were sold by public auction.

In 1883 the Eastern and Midlands Railway obtained an Act for a line between the GNR stations at Bourne and Little Bytham. It was to run from Bourne to Edenham, where they were empowered to purchase the route of Lord Willoughby's railway, together with its trackwork. This rather roundabout route would avoid the need to tunnel through the high ground due west of Bourne. His Lordship was not happy to see it incorporated into a through route over which he had no control, and to his satisfaction a later proposal saw the construction in 1893 of the direct Bourne/Little Bytham/Saxby line, with the necessary tunnel, which severed for ever the route of the erstwhile Edenham railway.

Figure 28.4   The trackbed, looking north from the roadbridge between Little Bytham and Witham on the Hill. The size of the trees growing there give a clue to the fact that no train had passed this way for ninety years   © Author

124

29

Essendine to Bourne

The Bourne and Essendine Railway opened on 16 May 1860, the first railway to reach Bourne, and gave ninety-one years of untroubled service, before becoming the first Lincolnshire line to be closed by British Railways.

This six-and-a-half-mile, single-track line was built by the Bourne and Essendine Railway Company to give Bourne a direct link with trains to and from London. It was a result of local initiative of the townspeople and it was worked by the Great Northern Railway (GNR) who retained half the income. It got off to an excellent start, £101 being taken in the first week, but it did not retain its independence for long, being taken over by the GNR in 1864.

At first there were two intermediate stations, the main one, with the only goods yard on the branch, at Thurlby, and the second, a platform only, at Braceborough Spa – surely one of the least known spas in England! In 1841 a bath house was built here, tapping a mineral spring which was considered beneficial for the treatment of skin diseases, and no doubt it was hoped that both the spa and the railway would benefit from the provision of a station. Although the bath house was still open on the eve of the Second World War, traffic was always low. Indeed, the London and North Eastern Railway (LNER) designated it a Class 6 station, and it had the distinction of being the lowest class staffed station in the Southern Area of the LNER. It became an unstaffed halt for a time on 19 February 1934, but it was later staffed again by a porter living in the Station House, who sold tickets and operated the level-crossing gates.

At a point almost a mile east of Braceborough Spa, the line passed a pumping station, built by the Peterborough Waterworks, which supplied the city with one million gallons of water per day. A siding to serve this was put in alongside the Wilsthorpe to Manthorpe road, and named Wilsthorpe Siding.

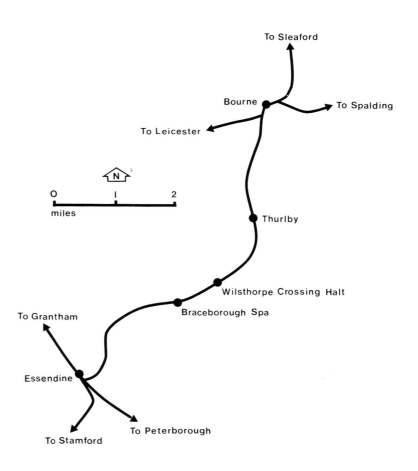

Figure 29.1 *Essendine to Bourne*

In the mid–1930s a halt was constructed here, Wilsthorpe Crossing Halt, the third, and final station on the line.

By 1887 Bourne Station was receiving trains from Kings Lynn via Spalding, and from Sleaford. At this time there were eight

Figure 29.2   *A lonely Braceborough Spa Station on 22 March 1968. Its isolated location is shown to the full. The road to the station ended there, and the level-crossing at the end of its platform gave access only to fields*   © Author

Table 73.   ESSENDINE AND BOURNE.

WEEKDAYS

		a.m.		a.m.	Th O a.m.		SO a.m.	Th O a.m.		SX p.m.	SO p.m.		p.m.		p.m.		p.m.	p.m.
LONDON (King's Cross) dep.		5 2		7 25	8 45		8 45			1130	1130	1640			3 0		4 15	5 50
Peterborough (North) — arr.		7 40		9 25	10 47		10 47			1 39	1 42	3 59			3 49		6 33	7 2
Essendine — — arr.		8 0		9 49	11 7		11 7			1 57	1 57	3 49			5 9		6 50	7 45
Grantham — — dep.		—		9 51	—		11 42	11 42		1 15	1 24	3 45			48 34		6 29	—
Essendine — — arr.		—		10 17	—		12 12	12 12		1 43	1 52	4 6			5 9		6 54	
ESSENDINE dep.		8 30		10 23	1115		1226	—	1 12		2 18	2 22	4 14			5 15	7 0	7 52
Braceborough Spa (Halt)		8 37		10 28	11 20		12 31	—			2 23	2 27	4 19			5 24	7 5	A
Wilsthorpe Crossing		8 42		10 32	11 24		12 35	—			2 27	2 31	4 23			5 24	7 9	A
Thurlby		8 47		10 35	11 27		12 38	—	1 23		2 30	2 34	4 26			5 27	7 12	A
BOURNE arr.		8 53		10 40	1132		1243	—	1 23		2 36	2 40	4 31			5 32	7 17	8 9

WEEKDAYS

		a.m.	a.m.	Th O p.m.		SO p.m.	Th O p.m.	Th X p.m.	Th O p.m.		p.m.		p.m.		p.m.	p.m.
BOURNE dep.		7 40	9 25	1047		12 3	1250	1 15	1 37		3 26		4 43		5 58	—
Thurlby		7 45	9 30	10 52		12 8	12 55	1 20	1 42		3 33		4 48		6 3	7 36
Wilsthorpe Crossing		—	9 34	10 56		12 12	12 59	1 24	—		3 37		4 52		6 11	7 38
Braceborough Spa (Halt)		7 50	9 37	10 59		12 15	1 2	1 27	—		3 40		4 56		A	A
ESSENDINE arr.		7 55	9 42	11 4		1220	1 7	1 32	1 52		3 45		5 0		6 24	7 46
Essendine — — dep.		8 1	9 51	11 9		1 27	—	1 58	1 58		3 50		5 11		6 51	7 49
Grantham — — arr.		8 34	10 35	11 42		2 2	—	2 23	2 22		4 11		5 41		7 15	8 20
Essendine — — dep.		8 54	10 19	12 23		12 23	1 44	1SX44	1SO53		4 18		5F10		6 56	9 15
Peterborough (North) — arr.		9 8	10 39	12 42		12 42	2 1	1SX 47	1SO47		4 40		5E29		7 10	9 23
LONDON (King's Cross) arr.		10 26	12 30			3 47	3SX47	3SO47			6 52		7 5		9 13	3 18

A Calls when required to set down on notice being given to the guard at the preceding stopping station.
B On Saturdays leaves Grantham 4.42 and arrives Essendine 5.14 p.m.
E On Saturdays runs 5 minutes later.

G On Saturdays until 14th September inclusive leaves King's Cross 1.50 p.m.
SO Saturdays only.
SX Saturdays excepted.
ThO Thursdays only.
ThX Thursdays excepted.

Figure 29.3   *An extract from the LNER timetable operative from 8 July to 29 September 1935. Note that almost all trains gave connections to and from London*
Courtesy Glenn Answer

trains each way between Essendine and Bourne, and three of these worked through from Kings Lynn. This situation continued until the Saxby extension from Bourne was opened by the Midland and Great Northern Joint Railway in 1894. For most of its life there were eight trains each way with two extra on Thursdays and Saturdays. In 1938 one Down train had no intermediate stops, one Up stopped only at Thurlby. Four stopped only if required at Braceborough Spa, otherwise all stopped at all stations.

After the formation of the LNER in 1923 all locomotive work-

Figure 29.4   *(On facing page) On the last day of service, 18 June 1951, an Essendine train pauses at Braceborough Spa Station. 2–6–0 No. 43058, was a Peterborough engine. The Guard is standing on the platform with a lady who may have been the wife of the Station Porter*   © G. Parkinson

ings were from Peterborough, New England depot, using either C12 4–4–2T or 0–6–0 tender engines. Their day began with the 4.0 am goods from Peterborough to Bourne. The engine then worked all passenger trains, Bourne to Essendine and back, finishing in Bourne at 8.29 pm, before taking the 9.15 pm goods to Peterborough, arriving 12.45 am. The first crew were relieved by a set based at Bourne who worked from 9.15 am to 5.40 pm, when a second New England crew took over after travelling as passengers to Bourne and finished the day's roster. From 1927 until closure the branch train was composed of an articulated twin set built out of two coaches from Ivatt steam-motor cars.

Complete closure came on 18 June 1951, with the traditional explosion of detonators placed on the line, and Lincolnshire people had their first opportunity since pre-war days to attend railway-closure celebrations.

Figure 29.5   The last passenger train to work over the branch waits at the Bourne platform at Essendine where a small group of people wait to watch the poignant scene. The engine is No 43062. The branch line can be seen curving away to the left immediately at the end of the platform　　　　　　　　© G Parkinson

Stamford to Essendine

The Great Northern Main Line, opened between Peterborough and Grantham in 1852 bypassed Stamford because, it is said, the 2nd Marquess of Exeter, the principal landowner, did not want the park associated with his home, Burghley Park, despoiled by the iron road.

Stamford was the terminus, for nineteen months, of the second railway built in Lincolnshire. This was the line from Peterborough, built by the Midland Railway, opened on 2 October 1846 and extended on to Melton Mowbray on 1 May 1848. The town then had a link with the Main Line to London from Peterborough, eleven-and-a-half-miles away. Whatever the reason for the Great Northern's not being allowed into Stamford, it is a fact that the town went into a decline which lasted until the turn of the century, the population falling by about nine per cent.

A better link with the Main Line was demanded, with the active support of the 2nd Marquess, and the Essendine and Stamford Branch was the result. Built by the Stamford and Essendine Railway Company, it was four miles long and single-line, and had one intermediate station at Ryhall and Belmesthorpe; it opened on 1 November 1856.

The company built their own terminal station, Stamford East, in Water Street. It had the appearance of a small Elizabethan mansion to harmonise with other buildings in the town. It had a single island platform, and a small, single-road, engine shed.

In an attempt to provide a better link with Peterborough, the company opened another line on 1 February 1867, eight-and-a-half miles to Wansford Station on the Peterborough to Northampton Line. These trains also ran from Stamford East Station, and together they became known as the Marquess of Exeter's Railways.

The Essendine Branch was worked by the Great Northern

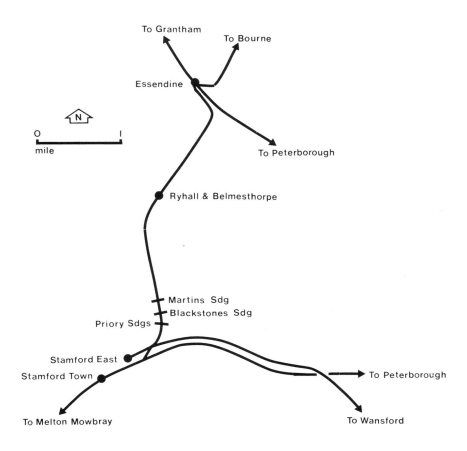

Figure 30.1 *Stamford to Essendine*

these being through trains from Wansford. The journey time from Stamford was ten minutes to Essendine and twenty-five to Wansford. A similar service was operated in 1914. In 1938, there were eleven each way daily, plus one extra on Saturday, and just one morning and one afternoon train on Sunday. Most trains connected with Main Line trains at Essendine.

In the latter half of the nineteenth century an important consideration in the determination of location of engineering industries was the location of a railway line, just as a hundred years before it had been a waterway, and a hundred years after, a motorway. Private sidings were laid from the branch to serve

Figure 30.3   *Stamford train at Essendine with Class C12 4–4–2T No 4508*
Courtesy E Neve collection

Figure 30.2   *The site of Ryhall and Belmesthorpe Station on 1 April 1974. This was once an attractive place, with a neat single-storey stone building at the far end of the platform and a wooden waiting room.*   © Author

Railway (GNR) until 1 January 1865, and again from 1 February 1872 and leased (by the GNR) from 15 December 1893. But in the period January 1865 to February 1872 the line was operated by the Marquess of Exeter and the Stamford and Essendine Railway Company, who purchased some second-hand carriages and two small locomotives from the London and North Western Railway. They also hired an additional locomotive from the GNR.

The service began with four trains each way daily, rising by 1864 to eleven trains each way, and by 1887 to fifteen, seven of

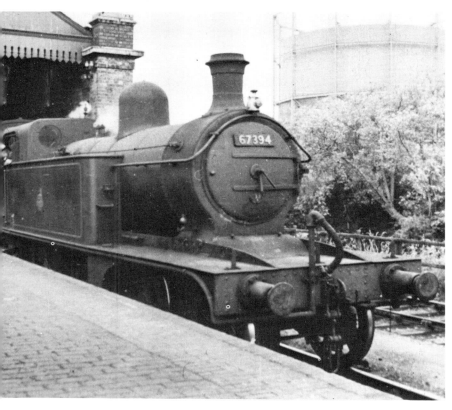

Figure 30.4   *Class C12 4–4–2T No 67394 waits at Stamford East on the morning of 5 July 1955 with an Essendine train. This engine, built in July 1907, was enjoying its 48th birthday. It was withdrawn three years later* © D Swift

Martin's Cultivator Works, Blackstone's Engineering Works and Stamford Priory Lime and Foundry. For almost a mile from East Station the line appeared to be double-track, but one was the single-track branch, the other a separate line to serve these three sets of sidings. In 1897, for example, there were three trains each way daily to serve these, and there were also four

Figure 30.5   *Another view of No 67394 taken at the same time as Figure 30.4. The island platform of Stamford East, with its overall roof and riverside location and with a tiny branch train, engine simmering gently in the summer sunshine evokes a scene now lost for ever. The other platform face was once used for trains to Wansford, but these ceased to run twenty-six years before* © D Swift

transfer goods trains each way between the Great Northern and Midland stations.

Trains to Wansford stopped running from 1 July 1929 when that branch closed. Even fifty-nine years ago there was too little traffic to justify the service. East Station closed on 4 March 1957 and trains were diverted into Town Station, although the East Station goods yard remained open until 4 March 1963.

The branch passenger service was lost altogether from 15 June 1959, and the line, together with Essendine Station, closed down for good. However, freight services continued to and from Priory Sidings until 27 November 1969.

Figure 30.6　Essendine Station on 22 May 1959 with an N5 0–6–2 tank waiting at the Stamford platform to take the 9.5 am to Stamford Town. When Stamford East Station closed in 1957, branch trains were diverted to the 'Town' station

© D Swift

31

Spalding to March

Conflict was the mark of history of this line, conflict between rival railway companies at the time of its opening, and management/staff conflict on its closure.

The Great Eastern Railway (GER) cast a covetous eye on the supply of Yorkshire's coal and manufactured goods to the capital. In 1863 they promoted a Bill for this line as their first step in establishing a suitable route. The Great Northern Railway (GNR) answered the move with a proposal of their own for the same line, and their stated intention for the transfer of goods between the companies at March won them the day. The nineteen-mile, double-track line was opened for goods on 1 April, and passengers on 2 August, both in 1867. Stations were provided at Cowbit, Crowland (renamed Postland from 1 December 1871), French Drove (renamed French Drove and Gedney Hill on 4 July 1938), Murrow and Guyhirne. A goods-only station was also built at Twenty Feet River, between Guyhirne and March. At Murrow the line crossed, on the level, the Peterborough, Wisbech and Sutton Railway, which had opened the previous year. A service of three trains each way was instituted.

The GER were not to be outsmarted, and in 1876 they proposed a Spalding–Lincoln line. Again the GNR did the same, and suggested that the Lincoln–March line be operated as a joint line. Agreement could not be reached and both Bills were placed before Parliament. The Great Northern Bill was passed with appropriate clauses to make it suitable as a joint line. Agreement was finally reached in 1879, and the line through to Lincoln was opened in 1882. From 1 August 1882, these lines, together with the existing GNR line from Lincoln to Doncaster, and a route south from March to St Ives in Huntingdonshire, the latter with branches to Ramsey and Huntingdon, became the Great Northern and Great Eastern Joint Railway, 122 miles

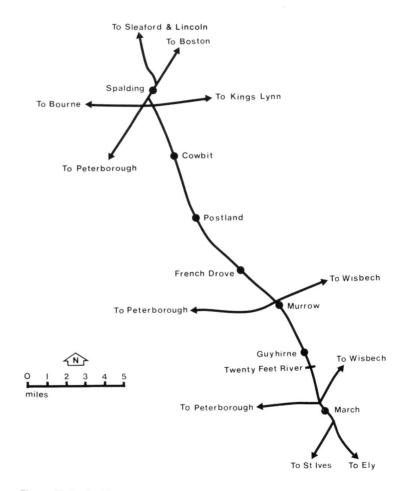

Figure 31.1 *Spalding to March*

Figure 31.2 *On 11 February 1961, a B1 locomotive pauses with a goods train to shunt wagons in the sidings at Cowbit. Exactly seven months later the station was to be closed for passengers, although goods trains continued to call until 1964*

© D Thompson

of line, linking Yorkshire with London.

The line always carried very heavy freight traffic, and to cope with this the GER enlarged its Whitemoor marshalling yard built alongside the Spalding–March line, north of March. In 1910 it held 1500 wagons and a hundred steam-engines were based there. By 1953 this had grown to four yards with a capacity for 7000 wagons.

General goods traffic was constant all year round. Additional traffic came to the line from horse-racing – trains of horseboxes with passenger coaches for the grooms travelled to and from Newmarket to racetracks such as Liverpool, Manchester, York, Doncaster, Ripon, Pontefract, Leicester and Birmingham. In its later years, after passenger trains ceased running between Peterborough and Sutton Bridge, a curve was put in at Murrow to give access to brickworks at Dogsthorpe and at Eye Green on the outskirts of Peterborough. Via this curve, for some years trains also ran to Wisbech North Station for fruit and vegetables, and to a branch to the harbour at this Cambridgeshire town, the former service ceasing on 18 April 1966, and the latter on 28 December 1964.

After the opening the GER ran a through service from London, Liverpool Street to Doncaster, extended from November 1892, to and from York, a distance of 212¾ miles. Until the outbreak of war in 1914 three weekday through trains operated over what the GER described as 'The Cathedrals Route', London/Ely/Lincoln and York. With numerous stops the journey took at least five hours twenty minutes. The service was not resumed after the war. A through boat-train commenced running in 1885 from Harwich to Doncaster. This too was extended to and from York in 1892. The best known train using the March–Spalding and Lincoln Line was undoubtedly the successor to this early boat-train. After the 1914–18 War it was diverted from York to serve Sheffield, Manchester and Liverpool Central, although York continued to be served by through coaches detached from the main train at Lincoln. This train also conveyed a section to and from Birmingham, detached at March to continue via Peterborough and the London, Midland and Scottish Railway. Until the withdrawal of steam in the area, Brittania Pacifics were used on this service and were a fine sight as they sped across the Fenland. This latter train was diverted via Peterborough in 1973, and some people saw this as a warning sign that a line-closure was in the offing

An interesting use of the line was the scheduling of summer-seasonal trains from northern cities to East Anglia. In 1938 these ran each way between Leeds, Norwich and Ipswich; Leeds, Lowestoft and Yarmouth; York, Lowestoft and Ipswich; Newcastle, Lowestoft and Yarmouth; Liverpool, Lowestoft and

Figure 31.3 *The 10.31 am Doncaster–Cambridge train (consisting of a Cambridge-based Craven-built, two-car multiple unit) about to pass over Twenty Feet River level-crossing. This was the penultimate southbound service train on the last day of the service, 27 November 1982. Behind the rear coach is the goods shed which at one time formed part of the goods yard here* © R E Burdon

Ipswich; Manchester and Clacton; and Sheffield and Felixstowe. Another annual period of great activity was the springtime Tulip Parade at Spalding with excursion trains from the south. These trains still run, but now via Peterborough. A little known feature of the line during the 1930s, in the peak summer season, was the 'Eastern Belle', a Pullman excursion from Liverpool Street via Cambridge and March to Skegness, which ran occasionally.

The local passenger service was always sparse. As we have seen, initially there were three trains each way. Seventy years later this had only risen to four each way a day. The Down and two Up trains in 1938 ran between March and Lincoln, calling at all stations. Two Up trains ran from Spalding to March. In 1953 both Murrow and Guyhirne stations were closed to passengers. On 11 September 1961 the three others were closed. By then they were served with only one passenger train each way a day.

Murrow lost its goods yard on 1 September 1947, and Cowbit, French Drove, and Guyhirne lost theirs on 5 October 1964. Postland, the last to close, went on 19 April 1965, and from this time no trains stopped anywhere between March and Spalding. In its final years, the line was travelled by passengers on three trains each way, travelling between Ely and Doncaster, and Norwich and Cambridge to York and Doncaster.

In 1982, British Rail announced their plan for closure of the March–Spalding line and for the diversion of all traffic between March and Spalding via Peterborough. Their argument was based on a projected road improvement on the A47 at Guyhirne which would involve increased cost if the line remained in use,

Figure 31.4 *The view south from the Welland Bridge at Spalding in January 1986. All the track had been removed from here towards Spalding Station, and the road reinstated over the level-crossings. A single line of overgrown track still remained towards March* © Author

135

and on their desire to save some £4 million on track-renewal on this line, together with the Lincoln- and Sleaford-avoiding lines. The date was set for 1 November 1982, but the Rail Unions were concerned about possible job losses at March because of what they saw as a growing desire to centralise the area's rail facilities at Peterborough, and the date was deferred.

Closure, however, could not be deferred for long and came on 29 November 1982 with 27 November being the last day of service. On this day, a man in a top hat and mourning dress was seen at Spalding, and the Fakenham and Dereham Railway Society organised a last farewell tour. On its return to March, the diesel multiple unit formed the last revenue-earning train.

There was still a final hiccup to come, however. In June 1983 there was a dispute between Guards and British Rail over the removal of the track – while the track remained there was some hope of restoration of services. The case of the now indispensable line from Peterborough to Spalding was cited to support the case for not removing the track – in the eight months between the time of its complete closure in 1970 and its reopening its traffic had actually grown. A compromise was reached, allowing one track to be removed, and the other to be left *in situ* for one year.

Alas, reopening did not come, and the line was severed at Spalding in the Spring of 1985. A short section north of March is retained to serve the still open Whitemoor Up yard. The Down yard closed on 27 January 1972 – a reflection of falling freight traffic – although it continued to be used for wagon storage until March 1976.

Figure 31.5 *A pair of Class 31 Brush diesel/electric locomotives, Nos 31.423 and 31.404, travelling northwards on the last day of scheduled services, 27 November 1982. This modern prefabricated signal box, with a forty-lever frame, replaced a more traditional one on 31 March 1974 which had become structurally unsafe. It controlled the exit from the Down yard at Whitemoor, and the entrance to the Up yard*
© R E Burdon

Appendix 1

Dates of opening and closure to both passenger and goods of stations and sidings on the railways described in this book

Station or Depot	Opened		Closed	
	Goods	*Passenger*	*Goods*	*Passenger*
Aby	3. 9.1848	3. 9.1848	11. 9.1961	11. 9.1961
Admiralty Platform Halt[5]		by 1921		17. 6.1963
Alford Town	3. 9.1848	3. 9.1848	2. 5.1966	5.10.1970
Alford[2]	2. 4.1884	2. 4.1884	12.1889	12.1889
Algarkirk and Sutterton	17.10.1848	17.10.1848	15. 6.1964	11. 9.1961
Aswarby and Scredington	10.1871	2. 1.1872	28. 7.1956	22. 9.1930
Authorpe	3. 9.1848	3. 9.1848	30. 3.1964	11. 9.1961
Bardney	17.10.1848	17.10.1848	3. 5.1965	5.10.1970
Belton	14.11.1904	2. 1.1905	5. 4.1965	17. 7.1933
Billingborough and Horbling	10.1871	2. 1.1872	15. 6.1964	22. 9.1930
Blacker Siding[1,3]	10. 8.1902		5. 4.1965	
Bourne	16. 5.1860	16. 5.1860	5. 4.1965	2. 3.1959
Braceborough Spa[4]	16. 5.1860	16. 5.1860	18. 6.1951	18. 6.1951
Burgh Le Marsh	3. 9.1848	3. 9.1848	2. 5.1966	5.10.1970
Burnham Lane Siding[3]	14.11.1904		1. 2.1956	
Castle Bytham	1. 5.1894	1. 5.1894	2. 3.1959	2. 3.1959
Caythorpe	15. 4.1867	15. 4.1867	15. 6.1964	10. 9.1962
Clenchwarton[1]	1.11.1864	1.11.1864	2. 3.1959	2. 3.1959
Clifton on Trent[1]	16.11.1896	15.12.1896	30. 3.1964	19. 9.1955
Coningsby[7]	1. 7.1913	1. 7.1913	30. 3.1964	5.10.1970
Cottam[1]	7. 8.1850	7. 8.1850	2.11.1959	2.11.1959
Counter Drain	1. 8.1866	1. 8.1866	30. 3.1964	2. 3.1959
Cowbit	1. 4.1867	2. 8.1867	5.10.1964	11. 9.1961
Cranwell	1917	1917	8.1956	1927
Crowle	10. 8.1902	10. 8.1902	5. 4.1965	17. 7.1933
Doddington and Harby[1]	16.11.1896	15.12.1896	30. 3.1964	19. 9.1955
Doddington Siding[1,3]	16.11.1896		30. 3.1964	
Dogdyke	17.10.1848	17.10.1848	17. 6.1963	17. 6.1963
Donington on Bain	27. 9.1875	27. 9.1875	1.12.1958	5.11.1951
Dukeries Junction[1,5]		1. 6.1897		6. 3.1950
Ealand Depot[3]	14.11.1904		5. 4.1965	
East Barkwith	9.11.1874	9.11.1874	1.12.1958	5.11.1951
East Halton Halt[4,8]		1. 5.1911		17. 6.1963
Eastoft[1]	10. 8.1902	10. 8.1902	5. 4.1965	17. 7.1933
Edenham	1855	8.12.1857	1873	1871
Epworth	14.11.1904	2. 1.1905	5. 4.1965	17. 7.1933
Eye Green[1]	1. 8.1866	1. 8.1866	18. 4.1966	2.12.1957
Ferry[1]	1. 8.1866	1. 8.1866	2. 3.1959	2. 3.1959
Firsby	3. 9.1848	3. 9.1848	7.12.1964	5.10.1970
Five Mile House[9]	17.10.1848	17.10.1848	15. 9.1958	15. 9.1958
Fledborough[1]	16.11.1896	15.12.1896	19. 9.1955	4. 1.1965
Fleet	1. 7.1862	1. 7.1862	3.12.1964	2. 3.1959
Fockerby	10. 8.1902	10. 8.1902	5. 4.1965	17. 7.1933
Fotherby Halt[5]		11.12.1905		11. 9.1961
French Drove and Gedney Hill	1. 4.1867	2. 8.1867	5.10.1964	11. 9.1961
Gedney	1. 7.1862	1. 7.1862	3.12.1964	2. 3.1959
Grainsby Halt[5]		11.12.1905		10. 3.1952
Great Coates Crossing[2]		15. 5.1912		1. 7.1961
Grimoldby	17.10.1877	17.10.1877	5.12.1960	5.12.1960
Grimsby, Cleveland Bridge[2]		15. 5.1912		1. 7.1961
Grimsby, Corporation Bridge[2]		15. 5.1912		1. 7.1956
Guyhirne[1]	1. 4.1867	2. 8.1867	5.10.1964	5.10.1953
Haconby Siding[3]	10.1871		5. 4.1965	
Hagg Lane Siding[3]	14.11.1904		5. 4.1965	
Hainton Street Halt[5]		11.12.1905		11. 9.1961
Hallington	26. 6.1876	1.12.1876	15. 9.1956	5.11.1951
Halton Holgate	1. 5.1868	1. 5.1868	1.12.1958	10. 9.1939
Harmston	15. 4.1867	15. 4.1867	10. 9.1962	10. 9.1962
Hatfield Moor[1,3]	22. 2.1909		30. 9.1963	
Haxey Junction	14.11.1904	2. 1.1905	1. 2.1956	17. 7.1933
Haxey Town	14.11.1904	2. 1.1905	1. 2.1956	17. 7.1933
Holbeach	3. 5.1858	3. 5.1858	5. 4.1965	2. 3.1959
Holton Le Clay	1. 3.1848	1. 3.1848	25. 5.1964	4. 7.1955
Holton Village Halt[5]		11.12.1905		11. 9.1961
Horncastle	11. 8.1855	11. 8.1855	5. 4.1971	13. 9.1954
Immingham Dock Western Jetty[6]		After 1918		Early 1930s
Immingham Town[2]		15. 5.1912		1. 7.1961
Killingholme Halt[10]	1.12.1910	1.12.1910	4. 1.1965	17. 6.1963
Kiln Lane, Stallingborough[2]		15. 5.1912		1. 7.1961
Kingthorpe	9.11.1874	9.11.1874	15. 9.1956	5.11.1951
Kirton	17.10.1848	17.10.1848	15. 6.1964	11. 9.1961
Langrick	17.10.1848	17.10.1848	17. 6.1963	17. 6.1963
Leadenham	15. 4.1867	15. 4.1867	15. 6.1964	1.11.1965
Legbourne Road	3. 9.1848	3. 9.1848	15. 6.1964	7.12.1953
Lincoln St Marks	3. 8.1846	3. 8.1846	3. 5.1965	12. 5.1985
Long Sutton	1. 7.1862	1. 7.1862	5. 4.1965	2. 3.1959
Louth	1. 3.1848	1. 3.1848	28.12.1980	5.10.1970
Ludborough	1. 3.1848	1. 3.1848	25. 5.1964	11. 9.1961
Luddington[1]	10. 8.1902	10. 8.1902	5. 4.1965	17. 7.1933

Station or Depot	Opened		Closed	
	Goods	Passenger	Goods	Passenger
Mablethorpe	17.10.1877	17.10.1877	30. 3.1964	5.10.1970
Midville[7]	1. 7.1913	1. 7.1913	30. 3.1964	5.10.1970
Milthorpe Siding[3]	10.1871		15. 6.1964	
Misson[1,3]	12. 8.1912		7.12.1964	
Morton Road	10.1871	2. 1.1872	5. 4.1965	22. 9.1930
Moulton	3. 5.1858	3. 5.1858	15. 6.1964	2. 3.1959
Mumby Road	4.10.1886	4. 10.1886	30. 3.1964	5.10.1970
Murrow East[1]	1. 8.1866	1. 8.1866	19. 4.1965	2. 3.1959
Murrow West[1]	1. 4.1867	2. 8.1867	1. 9.1947	6. 7.1953
Navenby	15. 4.1867	15. 4.1867	15. 6.1964	10. 9.1962
New Bolingbroke[7]	1. 7.1913	1. 7.1913	30. 3.1964	5.10.1970
New Holland Pier	1. 3.1848	1. 3.1848	5.11.1979	25. 6.1981
New Holland Town	1. 3.1848	1. 3.1848	5.11.1979	25. 6.1981
No 5 Passing Place[2]		15. 5.1912		1. 7.1961
Normanby Park[3]	1. 8.1912		Not known	
North Drove	1. 8.1866	1. 8.1866	30. 3.1964	15. 9.1958
North Thoresby	1. 3.1848	1. 3.1848	30.12.1963	5.10.1970
Postland	1. 4.1867	2. 8.1867	19. 4.1965	11. 9.1961
Reedness[1]	1. 1.1900	1. 1.1900	5. 4.1965	17. 7.1933
Rippingale	10.1871	2. 1.1872	15. 6.1964	22. 9.1930
Ryhall and Belmesthorpe[1]	1.11.1856	1.11.1856	15. 6.1959	15. 6.1959
Saltfleetby	17.10.1877	17.10.1877	5.12.1960	5.12.1960
Sandtoft Siding[3]	5. 1.1909		30. 9.1963	
Scunthorpe[14]	9.1906	9.1906	13. 7.1925	13. 7.1925
Skellingthorpe	16.11.1896	15.12.1896	30. 3.1964	19. 9.1955
Slea River Platform[5]		1917		1927
South Lynn[1, 11]	1.11.1864	1.11.1864		2. 3.1959
Southrey[7]	17.10.1848	17.10.1848	1.10.1955	5.10.1970
South Willingham	9.11.1874	9.11.1874	1.12.1958	5.11.1951
South Witham	1.5.1894	1.5.1894	6. 4.1964	2. 3.1959
Spilsby	1. 5.1868	1. 5.1868	1.12.1958	10. 9.1939
Stamford East	1.11.1856	1.11.1856	4. 3.1963	4. 3.1957
Stamford, Priory Sidings[3]	1.11.1856		27.11.1967	
Stickney[7]	1. 7.1913	1. 7.1913	30. 3.1964	5.10.1970
Stixwould[7]	17.10.1848	17.10.1848	17. 6.1963	5.10.1970
Surfleet	17.10.1848	17.10.1848	30.12.1963	11. 9.1961
Sutton Bridge	1. 7.1862	1. 7.1862	5. 4.1965	2. 3.1959
Sutton on Sea	4.10.1886	4.10.1886	30. 3.1964	5.10.1970
Sutton on Sea[2]	2. 4.1884	2. 4.1884	12.1889	12.1889
Tattershall	17.10.1848	17.10.1848	17. 6.1963	17. 6.1963
Terrington[1]	1.11.1864	1.11.1864	2. 3.1959	2. 3.1959
Theddlethorpe	17.10.1877	17.10.1877	5.12.1960	5.12.1960
Thorney[1]	1. 8.1866	1. 8.1866	28.12.1964	2.12.1957
Thorney and Wigsley Siding[1, 3]	16.11.1896		30. 3.1964	
Thurlby	16. 5.1860	16. 5.1860	18. 6.1951	18. 6.1951
Torksey	7. 8.1850	7. 8.1850	2.11.1959	2.11.1959
Tumby Woodside[7]	1. 7.1913	1. 7.1913	30. 3.1964	5.10.1970
Tuxford Central[1]	16.11.1896	15.12.1896	19. 9.1955	19. 9.1955
Twenty	1. 8.1866	1. 8.1866	30. 3.1964	2. 3.1959
Twenty Feet River[1,3]	1. 4.1867		13. 7.1964	
Tydd	1. 8.1866	1. 8.1866	2. 3.1959	2. 3.1959
Utterby Halt[5]		11.12.1905		11. 9.1961
Waddington	15. 4.1867	15. 4.1867	15. 6.1964	10. 9.1962
Walpole[1]	1.11.1864	1.11.1864	2. 3.1959	2. 3.1959
Waltham	1. 3.1848	1. 3.1848	15. 6.1964	11. 9.1961
Washingborough	17.10.1848	17.10.1848	29. 7.1940	29. 7.1940
Weelsby Road Halt[5]		11.12.1905		10. 3.1952
West Halton	9.1906	9.1906	29. 5.1961	13. 7.1925
Weston[4]	3. 5.1858	3. 5.1858	3. 2.1964	2. 3.1959
Whaplode[4]	3. 5.1858	3. 5.1858	3. 2.1964	2. 3.1959
Whitgift Siding[1, 3]	10. 8.1902		5. 4.1965	
Whitton	1.12.1910	1.12.1910	11.10.1951	13. 7.1925
Willoughby[12]	3. 9.1848	3. 9.1848	2. 5.1966	5.10.1970
Wilsthorpe Crossing Halt	early 1930s?	mid 1930s	18. 6.1951	18. 6.1951
Winteringham	15. 7.1907	15. 7.1907	11.10.1951	13. 7.1925
Winteringham Haven[3]	15. 7.1907		11.10.1951	
Winterton and Thealby	9.1906	9.1906	20. 7.1964	13. 7.1925
Wisbech North[1]	1. 8.1866	1. 8.1866	28.12.1964	2. 3.1959
Wisbech St Mary[1]	1. 8.1866	1. 8.1866	28.12.1964	2. 3.1959
Withcall	7.1882	1. 8.1882	15. 9.1956	5.11.1951
Woodhall Junction[13]	17.10.1848	17.10.1848	5. 4.1971	5.10.1970
Woodhall Spa	4. 4.1887	11. 8.1855	27. 4.1964	13. 9.1954
Wragby	9.11.1874	9.11.1874	1. 2.1960	5.11.1951
Wryde[1]	1. 8.1866	1. 8.1866	13. 7.1964	2.12.1957
Wymondham and Edmondthorpe[1]	1. 5.1894	1. 5.1894	3. 10.1960	2. 3.1959

NOTES

1 Not within the pre-1974 County of Lincolnshire
2 Tramway station
3 Goods station only
4 No sidings, goods dealt with from platform
5 Passenger station only
6 For boat trains only
7 Unstaffed from 7 October 1968
8 Unstaffed from 2 August 1948
9 Weekend anglers' trains continued to call to 6 September 1964
10 Unstaffed from 1 September 1956
11 Yard still in use for coal
12 New station, 130 yards north, from 4 October 1886
13 Unstaffed from 4 November 1968
14 North Lindsey Light Railway

Dates refer to public use only, private sidings are not included. These are the official closure dates: those given in the text may vary and, if so, the latter is the date the last train ran.

Appendix 2

List of pre-1974 Lincolnshire stations and public sidings, now closed, on lines still in use.

Appleby	Helpringham	Pinchbeck
Barkston	Holton le Moor	Potterhanworth
Blotoft Siding	Honington	Quadring Siding
Bloxholme Siding	Hougham	Reepham
Blyton	Howsham	Scawby and Hibaldstow
Branston and Heighington	Langworth	Scopwick and Timberland
Claxby and Usselby	Lea	Seacroft
Claypole	Little Bytham	Sedgebrook
Corby Glen	Little Steeping	Sibsey
Digby	Littleworth	Snelland
Donington Road	Moortown	St James Deeping
Eastville	Nocton and Dunston	Stow Park
Godknow Bridge	North Kelsey	Tallington
Gosberton	Northorpe	Thorpe on the Hill
Great Ponton	Old Leake	Ulceby Aerodrome Platform
Haxey and Epworth	Peakirk	Wickenby

Appendix 3

List of pre-1974 Lincolnshire stations, still open for passengers, but which have lost their public goods sidings.

Ancaster	Great Coates	Skegness
Barnetby	Habrough	Spalding
Barton on Humber	Havenhouse	Stallingborough
Brigg	Healing	Stamford Town
Brocklesby	Heckington	Swinderby
Cleethorpes	Hubberts Bridge	Swineshead Bridge
Crowle	Hykeham	Thornton Abbey
Elsham	Kirton Lindsey	Thorpe Culvert
Gainsborough Central	Market Rasen	Ulceby
Gainsborough Lea Road	Rauceby	Wainfleet
Goxhill	Saxilby	

Principle Sources and References

Balfour, B (1981) *The Armoured Train*, Batsford, London.

Clinker, C R (1971) *Clinker's Register of Closed Passenger Stations and Goods Depot, 1830–1970*, published by the author.

Dow, G (1984) *The Alford and Sutton Tramway*, published by the author.

Hancock, T N (1978) *Bomber County*, Lincolnshire Recreational Services, Lincoln.

Leleux, R (1984) *A Regional History of the Railways of Great Britain, Vol. 19: The East Midlands*, David & Charles, Newton Abbot.

Parker, S (1984) *The Edenham and Little Bytham Railway*.

Robinson, D N (1983) *The Book of Horncastle and Woodhall Spa*, Barracuda Books, Chesham.

Robinson, D N (1981) *The Book of the Lincolnshire Seaside*, Barracuda Books, Chesham.

Squires, S E (1987) *Lincolnshire Potato Railways*, Oakwood Press, Headington, Oxford.

Wright, N R (1982) *Lincolnshire Towns and Industry, 1700–1914*, History of Lincolnshire Committee.

Wrottesly, J (1981) *Great Northern Railway Vol. III*, Batsford, London.

Magazines

East Midlands Geographer
Lincolnshire Industrial Archaeology Newsletter
Lincolnshire Life
Lincolnshire Transport Review
Railway Magazine
Railway World
Steam Railway
Trains Illustrated

Newspapers

Grantham Journal
Grimsby Evening Telegraph
Lincolnshire Echo
Lincolnshire Free Press
Lincolnshire Standard Group
Stamford Mercury

Libraries

Doncaster Central
Gainsborough
Grantham
Grimsby Public
Lincoln Central
Lincolnshire Archives
RAF College, Cranwell

Museums

Museum of Army Transport, Beverly
Goxhill Railway Museum
Imperial War Museum
National Railway Museum
Rutland Railway Museum
Scunthorpe Museum

Miscellaneous

British Rail, Immingham Dock
British Steel, Scunthorpe
Grimsby Louth Railway Preservation Society
Midland and Great Northern Railway Society
Great Northern Railway Society

Index

Page numbers that are set in bold face denote photographs